DANCING AT THE CASTLE

Dancing at the Castle

Growing Up in Old Saybrook

JANE M. GULLONG

All photographs, unless otherwise indicated, are courtesy of the author.

Editor: Mike Urban

Cover and interior design: Vicky Vaughn Shea, Ponderosa Pine Design

For Dot and Bud

Contents

Growing Up in Old Saybrook

Once upon a time Old Saybrook was the most glamorous place on earth. Striped, canvas-slung beach chairs lay in the little yards. There was dancing at the Castle. We drove big Buicks with white fins, and our rich relatives had a cabin cruiser. We waited for the high tides of early September for one last swim. Lighthouses marked the shore, and there was crabbing in the creeks. The place was alive with celebrities. Katharine Hepburn was at home in Fenwick. A movie starring Doris Day was being shot in nearby Chester, and it was even named for me, *It Happened to Jane*. Troy Donohue came to Essex to make *Parrish*. We were on the straw-hat circuit, so I dressed up in my Fair Isle sweater and went to matinees with my mother at the Ivoryton Playhouse.

Old Saybrook was the place where I grew up. We called it "Down the Shore" long before I had moved to New York, where they think the shore is down in New Jersey. This is the place where I learned to work.

Waitressing was a virtual internship for my career in fundraising, where customer relations was the key to a good tip and later a generous contribution.

Old Saybrook was the place that I left to make my way in the wider world. But I returned as a daughter, a mourner, a caregiver, and a sister. And I am returning again to remember the place on Long Island Sound where the story of my life began.

At the wheel of a small fiberglass speedboat, entering the mouth of the Connecticut River at age 16, I was a Valkyrie with the wind in my face and my eyes on the red bell buoy to starboard. Flying along the breakwater between the outer and inner lighthouses, I was the captain of my tiny craft. Old Saybrook was ground zero on the compass. I was beginning to chart my own course, eager to fly free with yet no thought of what it would mean to return again and again.

Growing up in Old Saybrook meant not only coming of age, but watching my parents grow old, leaving them once, and then later again forever. Growing up in Old Saybrook, bathed in its glamour, its romance, and its sunsets, I have never been able to completely leave its shore.

Kate and Me

Like me, Katharine Hepburn kept Old Saybrook figuratively on her right, a home place where she would and could always return. When her voice in the PBS documentary trembles, "I wanted to get back to Old Saybrook," our town gets its place in the history of Hollywood royalty.

Katharine Hepburn was from Hartford, like many of us who spent summers in Old Saybrook. Like my family, hers made trips down the shore, theirs probably in a sporty 1913 touring car, mine in a white-winged 1959 Buick.

The summer life of the Hepburn family in Fenwick, a borough of Old Saybrook, is resonant of the fun, the games, the visitors, and the conflicts that so many of us remember in Old Saybrook summers of our own. We love celebrities for their glamorous lives, so different and remote from ours. But we love them all the more for all that we have in common.

Seeing Kate was a sport in Old Saybrook. We saw her

in Patrick's Country Store buying flannel shirts (she was the only woman in New England who looked good in one). We saw her coming out of Miss James's Pharmacy. We saw her on the golf course at Fenwick. Seeing Katharine Hepburn was like sighting a rare bird—an osprey, a crane—glimmering with celebrity in the tall grasses off Saybrook Point.

The golf course at Fenwick, open to the public, must be among the tiniest and prettiest little golf courses in New England—nine holes, most of them with views of Long island Sound, the grand Fenwick cottages, or the north cove of the Connecticut River. On a rise you can see the inner and outer lighthouses. But the prize was seeing Kate swinging a club before returning to her rambling, white waterfront house.

Even better was a chance to hear her remarkable familiar voice. The voice was at once moneyed, New Englandy, actressy, Philadelphia-y and icy cool. But it was always wavering on the edge of a deep-veiled emotion, even if she was only ordering cold cuts at Walt's Market.

For the most part we left her alone. We knew that good fences made good neighbors. There was a sign at the head of the dirt road to her house in Fenwick that could only have been composed by the clear-spoken Kate herself: "Please Go Away." Just in case you didn't understand "No Trespassing." Most everyone in Old Saybrook did keep out. But we kept watching.

Katharine Hepburn was never my favorite movie

star. I liked Elizabeth Taylor and Rosalind Russell. I liked their warm, dark sexiness. When I was 13, I had their pictures on the dividing wall of my room upstairs at our cottage on Cornfield Point. Kate was cool and a little disdainful, a little too reminiscent of my own mother, a girl from northern Maine. By the time Kate was the right age to star in *On Golden Pond,* I started to appreciate her virtues. Her loyalty, tenacity, and courage reminded me of my mother as well.

The Hepburn family bought their original house in Fenwick in 1913, around the same time that our cottage on Cornfield Point was built. Dr. Hepburn, Katharine's father, is said to have called Fenwick "Hartford on the rocks." My own witty father named our cottage The Breakers, a reference to the price, the surf, and the mansion in Newport.

Dr. Thomas Hepburn was a urologist specializing in venereal disease, and his wife, Kit, was a suffragette, working first for the women's vote then as an advocate for birth control. Still Hep and Kit didn't approve of Kate's interest in the theater, just as my parents, Dot and Bud Gullong, took a dim view of my move to New York City to work in the arts.

Like me, Katharine Hepburn brought her friends and lovers home to Old Saybrook. She drove up with her college girlfriends from Bryn Mawr. She drove up from New York with her future husband, Luddy Smith, in his Ford Model A. Once she was working in Hollywood, her beaus were increasingly legendary. Kate brought to Old

Saybrook the hard-drinking, gifted director John Ford. Howard Hughes flew Kate to Connecticut from Hollywood, tipping the wings of his plane over the house at Fenwick. And yes, Spencer Tracy made at least one trip to Fenwick. My boyfriends visited, but they pale in comparison.

Like me, she found work nearby. Kate performed one season at the Ivoryton Playhouse. One summer I was the social director of the Castle Inn.

Kate returned to Old Saybrook to live towards the end of her life. She could be seen chopping wood at age 75 and swimming in Long Island Sound even in January. At Fenwick she worked on her memoirs on the porch and looked out at the same view she had been enjoying for nearly 100 years.

As I worked on my own memoir, I was able to follow the fortunes of (and a fortune it would take to buy) Kate's beloved property on Zillow and Trulia. (The house recently sold for $11.5 million.) But if you want to remember what Fenwick was like for Kate—comfy, cottagey, rag-tag, and hamish—find a copy of the 2004 Sotheby's catalog for the auction of her estate. Here are the well-used pine wooden tables, stools bought while filming *The African Queen,* wicker, wrought-iron lamps, needlepoint runners, scuffed-up wooden golf clubs, and best of all, her own paintings and drawings.

Not surprisingly, her leitmotif was the view from her windows of our beloved Old Saybrook lighthouses.

Katharine Hepburn on the beach at Fenwick. (archive photograph)

The Summer of 1944

The story of my life in Old Saybrook begins on Indianola Drive in Cornfield Point, circa August 1944 in my grandfather's yellow cottage.

My father, Charles Eli Gullong, nicknamed "Bud," was home from the war. With a medical discharge for flat feet, he left his destroyer, the USS *Foote*, in the Pacific for a reunion with my mother, Dorothy Small Gullong. Among his genetic gifts to me are a complete absence of arches and an interest in storytelling. He was always ready to have a laugh of gratitude about his feet going flat on the decks of the *Foote*. In fact, it was no laughing matter, since a mere two weeks after his discharge, a torpedo hit the *Foote*, killing all the men at Dad's former station.

My mother, Dorothy, nicknamed "Dot," had been waiting for Dad in Berlin, Connecticut, where she was a teacher and dean of girls at Berlin High School. She also worked part time at Fafnir Ball Bearing, supporting the war effort. Mom had grown up in Mars Hill, Maine, far north in Aroostook County, and migrated to central Connecticut in her 30s, still unmarried. In 1940s America she was well on her way to old maidhood. Dad always said he "saved her from a fate worse than death." Hmmm.

Married in June 1942, they were too soon parted, with America already at war with Germany and Japan. My father left New York harbor on his way to the *Foote* the following August. In my lifetime my parents seldom visited New York. But this time, on the eve of Dad's shipping out, they stayed together in Room 13 (their lucky number forever after) of a midtown hotel. I once came upon some letters sent by my father to my mother through the military postal service. "The ship leaves tomorrow. We don't know where we are going. Hope to be home soon. Love, Bud." In the middle of the Pacific, American troops were moving in secret without cellphones, Internet, or Skype. My father's handwritten message, a few plain words, seemed to me a love letter most powerful.

Once home, they couldn't wait to get down the shore to Dad's father's (Gramp's) cottage at Cornfield Point. Even though blackout curtains were still drawn on windows facing Long Island Sound, the Pease House was open and Ye Castle Inn was just a walk up the street. The music was Tommy Dorsey, the Ink Spots, Bing Crosby, and Dinah Shore. The songs: "I'll Be Seeing You," "That Old Black Magic," "I'll Get By, As Long As I Have You." Dot and Bud were great dancers. On the dance floor their daily lives slipped away, and they became cosmopolitans, lovers, Fred and Ginger, Nick and Nora Charles.

Their reunion must have been both joyous and passionate. I, Jane Meredith Gullong, was born on April 19, 1945.

Gramp's cottage was my first Old Saybrook retreat. It was an alluring place for a child. I remember crawling on the dirt underneath the house, Alice in a wonderland of beach chairs, garden tools, umbrellas, and metal sand pails. A dark, dusty model of a frigate loomed on the mantel of the house's huge beach stone fireplace. Not only could I crawl under the house, I could see over the walls, following the whiff of Noxema to see my cousin Peggy smear it on her sunburned nose in the bathroom. Lying in bed, I would fall asleep under the exposed eaves of the roof, full of knots and knicks that looked like faces and animals in the wood, a menagerie of the imagination.

Gramp and Nana must have driven down to Old Saybrook in their first car in 1925 to find Cornfield Point, a new development on the Connecticut shore. Building lots were divided up from the former estate property called "Hartlands," owned by the Beach family, and the mansion there soon became the Castle. The tiny lots were thickly settled, but their houses were individually designed and built. Their diversity lent charm. These were real cottages, many built by families themselves (my teenage father and his friends helped my grandfather build his), using stones from the shore for fireplaces and foundations.

I was not the first prodigal child in the Gullong

family. They all came from elsewhere. I can only imagine the motivations and the courage it took for each of their journeys. My mother moved alone from the potato fields of Aroostook County, Maine, to teach in Berlin, Connecticut. Uncle David Lieberman left an urban hospital in his native Brooklyn to set up a practice in Chester, Connecticut, where Jewish names were few and far between. Even Dad, who was rooted in Connecticut, had run away to sea, joining the Merchant Marine aboard the cargo steamer *Oriente* bound for Havana, before World War II took him to the Pacific.

Nana and Gramp (Margaret Heilener and Charles Gullong) came circa 1920 to Berlin, Connecticut, a very long way from the coal-rich valley of their birth and teenage marriage in Pottsville, Pennsylvania. They left behind huge families, bringing memories of their Pennsylvania Dutch speech inflections and a great grandmother called "Gros Mama." Gramp worked for the Berlin Construction Company, building bridges all over the Northeast. Nana was a staunch Methodist, a source of strength, wisdom, and the German potato salad, which became a staple of summers on Cornfield Point. Here's the recipe:

Pennsylvania Dutch Hot Potato Salad

8 medium potatoes

4 eggs

1½ teaspoon salt

2 tsp. black pepper

½ cup sugar

¼ cup Heinz cider vinegar, diluted with ¼ cup water

3-4 slices of bacon

1 onion, chopped

Boil the potatoes in their skins until soft.

In a bowl, beat the eggs with a fork, then add the above ingredients, except the potatoes, bacon, and onions.

Cut the bacon in ¼-inch pieces. Fry until crisp in a Dutch oven or heavy pot.

Add the ingredients from the bowl to the bacon pieces and fat, stirring steadily as it cooks and thickens.

Pour the mixture over warm potatoes. Add the chopped onion and stir gently until blended.

Sadly, I hardly knew these grandparents. In fragments of memory and in photographs, they are always dressed up—Nana wearing black tie shoes holding her pocketbook in front of her like the Queen of England, Gramp in a white shirt with suspenders, smoking a pipe. And in my favorite photo, Gramp is in his Spanish-American War uniform, a skinny teenager in 1898 looking hardly battle-ready. Did they ever don bathing suits, go to the beach at Cornfield Point, and swim?

Their oldest child also left home. Cathryn Gullong went to the Methodist Hospital in Brooklyn, New York,

Gramp   Nana

for nurses' training in 1925. She was distracted there by a handsome doctor, David Leonard Lieberman, and they were married in June 1928. My Uncle Davie's parents sat shiva.

Living in Brooklyn, New York, Katie and Dave loved to come to Old Saybrook, and I love to look at the photos of all of them at Gramp's cottage. My father is standing at the end of the jetty, wearing dapper white sporting clothes. Cathryn, my Aunt Katie, whom I remember as the stout, teetotaling matriarch of our family, sits in a bathing suit, cross-legged on the beach, her braided hair

Aunt Katie   Dad

wound round the top of her head and a twinkle in both her eyes. It was 1944 and magical to be at Cornfield Point.

These two newly married couples in their 30s (my mother must have been the photographer, since I have no images of her at Cornfield Point in the 1940s) were setting out on a life that would become centered in Old Saybrook for the next 50 years.

I, too, was soon beginning my life in Old Saybrook. The Cornfield Point beach was the setting for photo shoots,

Me, building castles in the sand on Cornfield Point Beach.

where my fabulous outfits and emerging charms were put on display. This is the same beach where a decade later I gathered daily with the boys and girls of my first teenage summer at the shore. I had already learned to flirt.

Gramp's yellow cottage stood virtually unchanged on its rise at Indianola Drive well into the 21st century. But suddenly in 2010, it disappeared into a giant new house. All over Cornfield Point, where little cottages once nestled, big enough for honeymooning and opening clams on the back porch, houses were growing to the size of their lots, air conditioned, with plastered ceilings and finished basements. With no way to crawl under the floors or see over the walls, they are nice but no place for the imagination.

First Gullong cottage on Cornfield Point.

Gramp's cottage at Cornfield Point was the place where memory began for me. It was where the soft sand, the rough barnacled jetties, the rhythm of the tides, the brine of the breeze, and the curve of the creeks were imprinted upon me as home. Like my family, I would leave home, leave them and Old Saybrook behind . . . for a while.

First I had to pass eight years landlocked in the middle of Connecticut. Wethersfield, a pretty suburb of Hartford, was best known then as the site of the Connecticut State Prison. For my dad, the town's most treasured feature was Wethersfield Cove, a quiet aquatic cul-de-sac of the Connecticut River, not far from our house at 352 Church Street. It was a reminder that like the river, we were not far from the Long Island shore, connected by a short, 37-mile drive to Old Saybrook.

Driving Down
The Shore

The 1950s were a quiet time in America. Mom and Dad were a silent majority of their own, too busy to talk much; and I, a child, was encouraged to be seen and not heard. In our family much was left unsaid. The cottage in Old Saybrook and Nana and Gramp seemed to disappear. Whether shielded or deprived, I was not aware that Nana and Gramp had died, nor did I share what my parents must have suffered with their loss.

There are snatches of real memories: Gramp with his head of thick, pure white hair sitting in his rocking chair in the kitchen smoking his pipe. Gramp in his garden surrounded by peonies taller than me. Gramp setting off Roman candles in the back yard of the house in Kensington. Sitting beside Nana in a pew of the Methodist church. The happiness I felt when she praised me for being "good in church" and wrapped her age-spotted arm around me. A drawer full of black-and-white pictures at the bottom of the stairs. Nana standing in the sunroom holding a present for me behind her back.

Their black sedan with a running board was parked in the driveway, ready for their trip down the shore. This tradition, the drive down the river, down old Route 9, down the shore, is embedded in the histories of so many Connecticut families.

For us, the drive began in Wethersfield, Connecticut, where we lived in a Dutch colonial house at 352 Church Street. In Wethersfield I graduated from high school, grew from childhood to college student, and saw many of my friends marry in the Congregational Church. But Wethersfield was the place for work and winter weather. All the glamour and allure and all the fun were down the shore.

It would begin with Dad calling up the stairs to my brother Bart and me. "Hey, you kids. Get into your fighting clothes. Do you want to take a little ride? We're going down the shore."

Quickly dressed in our dungarees (aka jeans) and well-worn flannel shirts, we were in our fighting clothes and scrambling into the car for our Saturday magic carpet ride. The car was a huge, gorgeous, white 1959 Buick with angled fins, the perfect chariot to carry us to Old Saybrook. In our family fairy tale, the visor mirror on Mom's side of the front seat read not "Who's the Fairest of them All?" but "Buick is a Beauty, too." A cauldron of family life, the Buick held the four of us on a journey from which we children had as yet no escape. In the big back seat we were without seat belts or video screens. We were free to fight, whine, and dream, looking out the window while looking forward to getting out.

Like an Indian path, old Route 9, now scenic Connecticut Route 154, winds and turns through the Connecticut River valley from Hartford to Old Saybrook. In Middletown we would catch our first glimpse of the Connecticut River. Mother never failed to remark that we were passing through sacred ground, the place where my brother, Bart, and I were born in 1945 and 1948 in Middlesex Hospital.

We looked eagerly for the swinging bridge to Portland on the other side of the river and for the famous "Come On Over" sign on a factory façade there. We never made the crossing. I would start to softly sing "Sailing Down the River On a Sunday Afternoon." My brother, three years younger, practiced boos and catcalls.

A picnic at Seven Falls roadside rest area in Haddam set us free from the car's back seat to clamor along the pine-needle-laden paths, trip over gnarled roots, and run along the brook with its seven miniature cascades of water.

Mom would snag a table under the shadiest trees and take the thermos and picnic basket out of the trunk of the car. The thermos full of sweetened ice tea was an army-issue-sized jug with a spigot. The basket, a shellacked lattice box with double handles, was full of ham and pickle sandwiches on white bread. Fig Newtons were there for dessert. Here's the recipe for ham and pickle sandwiches:

Ham and Pickle Sandwiches

Finely chop 2 cups baloney or ham (or use a Fafnir meat grinder)

Mix with 3 tablespoons green relish (with high fructose corn syrup)

Add ⅓ cup (or to taste) mayonnaise

Spread mixture on white bread

Tightly wrap individual sandwiches in saran to assure slightly soaked bread

Or we might stop and pick up grinders at Bennie's in Centerbrook. A Bennie's grinder is neither hoagie nor hero nor sub. It is the one and only stack of provolone and pepper-laced genoa salami on a long, white roll slathered in oil, vinegar, tomatoes, and shredded lettuce, cut in three pieces, and wrapped in waxed paper. I can gain a pound just thinking about them. My brother was long the self-appointed spokesperson for Bennie's, spreading the news of the deliciousness of this grinder far and wide.

Also along the river, the town of Chester was a landmark because Dad's sister Cathryn, my Aunt Katie, had settled there with her husband, the doctor whom she had met in nurses' training at Brooklyn Methodist Hospital. In Chester, Uncle Davie had set up a country doctor general practice, the only doctor in this small town.

Throughout his life, Dr. Lieberman made house calls, carrying a black leather bag with a stethoscope peeking out of the top. Their grand, yellow Victorian house was made for hide and seek. There was a summer room walled in stained glass and full of plants, secret back stairs to the kitchen, and a third floor attic leading to a tower turret full of old snowshoes, skates, and sleds.

We children could get easily lost playing in the house, especially if the visit was going to include a trip to the medical office suite off the kitchen. There, the icy-cold stethoscope might befall our chests and the dreaded wooden *ahhh* sticks might hold down our tongues for a peek down our throats. Luckily we were a healthy lot, and these forays usually ended with no more than an aspirin

Lieberman house, West Main Street, Chester, Connecticut.

and a hard pinch on the cheek, one of Uncle Davie's special gestures of affection. But the best thing that ever happened back there was when Uncle Davie pierced my ears. Once I accepted the sterile conditions, Mom was resigned to what she considered my mad desire to become a gypsy.

Our eye doctor, Bob Potts, was also on the route to the shore in a large, commanding house just past the ivory factory in Deep River. There in the 1950s he dispensed my white, cat-eyed glasses, which looked quite a bit like the Buick.

Essex, the beautiful gem of a village, home to sea captains and the historic Griswold Inn, was a tempting detour. Leaving Deep River in front of the Congregational Church, we would often take the River Road to the left towards Essex, glimpsing the river between the houses and trees.

In the summer we might find our Lieberman cousins, Leonard and Peggy, and Aunt Katie and Uncle Dave at Essex's steamboat dock. We loved to walk down the dock, past the "Owners Only" sign to the slip where their beautiful cabin cruiser the *Candy II* was tied up and find the Liebermans sitting in the stern.

But we could never stay long, since we were bound for Old Saybrook, and soon we were back on Route 154. Just entering Old Saybrook, there was a forest, thinned now, developed in recent years as Obed Heights, but this thicket of trees was the cool gateway to Old Saybrook. The temperature dropped, and Mom would always say,

"Ahh, just smell the salt air."

Finally in Old Saybrook, there were the must-do's—mandatory roads and places that we had to find the time to at least swing by. Main Street with its center esplanade welcomed and beckoned us to drive straight to the river. We looked for the quick left onto North Cove Road to cruise along Old Saybrook's little gold coast. Historic houses line the cove and look out at the rocking masts of the boats moored in this first safe harbor on the river. We might pause to take in the view at the parking spot (later in my teens referred to as the place to "watch submarine races") or drive on to historic Saybrook Point.

After lunch or a walk on the docks, we would drive across the narrow causeway. Always on the right was a flotilla of swans in South Cove and on the left glimpses of the lighthouses. The causeway esplanade provides a beautiful walkway for modest exercise with river and cove views. Walkers share the path with fishing families, many of the senior members stretched out in small lawn chairs while the youngsters tend white plastic buckets swirling with sea robins and the occasional fluke.

Just off the causeway we watched for a favorite left turn, the unmarked road into the borough of Fenwick. Turning in, we would wind around the weathered shingled mansions, confident in Dad's knowledge that the golf course and the roads were open to the public. We passed by the "Please Go Away" sign marking the dirt road to Katharine Hepburn's house but always turned down the "Residents Only" path along the river to the

Inner Light. Dad said he looked like he belonged. (Except for the kids in their fighting clothes in the backseat.)

But whether we came the other way flying along Great Hammock Road past Town Beach or following Maple Avenue with its expansive view across Long Island Sound, we always ended up at Cornfield Point. We would cruise by Gramp's cottage, then drive under the portico in front of the Castle.

Once, when I was 13, the car suddenly stopped in front of a cottage on West Shore Drive right beside the Cornfield Point beach, and Dad said, "We're home."

The Breakers: Gullong Cottage on Cornfield Point Beach

O ur cottage, the first to be built on Cornfield Point, faced west where each evening the twilight sky lit up our summers with fiery colors. It sat above a tiny private beach with its own surf-splashed boulder. I sat on its barnacled slope, brooding and dreaming my teens away. If ever we were a family, it was here. If ever we were a happy family, it was there. We weren't the Hepburns, but we had our stories.

First there were the drinks. My father was not much of a drinker. In fact often before going out to a party, he would drink a glass of milk to coat his stomach and slow the absorption of alcohol. Still the story went that Dad had a couple of drinks, Manhattans, straight up his usual, and suddenly found himself buying the cottage at 1 West Shore Drive. With savings shot and waves crashing on our rocky beach, Dad named our new home after the great Newport cottage, The Breakers.

Something vestigial arose in my father as he took possession of his shorefront lot. It was his territory. Set beside the sandy association swimming beach, it tempted trespassers. But the property had deeded riparian rights, meaning that we owned the beach all the way to the tideline. While the Hepburn sign over in Fenwick simply said "Please Go Away," Dad posted an esoteric message regarding riparian rights. Trespassers, justly confused, honored it mostly in the breach. Dad, like an early ancestor at the mouth of his cave, took delight in barking at the interlopers.

As legal proprietor of the beach all the way to the tideline, Dad took personal responsibility for its navigability. He had no need for a gym when there were rocks to be thrown—a true Sisyphean project, clearing the path—throwing the largest stones to the left and right, aiming to hit sand. Along this path in rubber shoes, we could swim out to our private mooring or carry our dinghy up to its berth on the sand. That is, until the next storm hit and Dad's salty, barnacled quarry was repositioned as nature originally intended.

As a teenager Dad paddled his canoe off this very beach. Now the head of a family, he was in firm possession of a piece of it. Once he secured its boundaries, another side of Dad's nature kicked in: the host. He made our cottage the most inviting site on the shore. The Breakers might have been the deck of an ocean liner, festooned as it was with flags and searchlights, visible for miles around. Here reflected perfectly in the life he made for our family at Cornfield Point was the Dad I knew, at times the brooding, angry introvert casting stones, at other times, the shining glad-hander, warm and welcoming.

The cottage sat on a slab of concrete, a patio decorated with life rings salvaged from a Pease House auction, lobster buoys found on Maine beaches, and handmade (by Dad) wooden sailboat plaques. There was a mysterious sign carved "Fiddler's Green." Aluminum lounge chairs, cross-hatched with pink and black nylon and light and easy to carry, were scattered around. Several large black inner tubes were available for surfing as well as a strong canvas raft, which had to be blown up annually with a bicycle pump.

The Breakers.

"Cottage style" got its start inside The Breakers. A full set of wicker furniture, painted burnt gold and covered in rusty red fabric printed with a fleet of tall sailing ships, filled the living room in front of the field-stone fireplace. Mom sat in the rocker, and Dad commandeered the lounge. There were two downstairs bedrooms—one where Mom and Dad slept in a double bed and a guest room where I loved to fall asleep listening to the adults talking in the living room. For me, they were the leaders of the free world, and I wanted to know what they were saying.

Upstairs off an open center room with beds nestled under the eaves, my room was a sanctuary and a lookout station. With a view of the beach and the road above it, I could track the comings and goings of all the kids of Cornfield Point. Soon I would be hanging out with them, in and out of love (or like) with most.

Family life at the cottage had many rituals. Foremost among them were the flags. Holidays were marked with full regalia—a display of colorful navy-issue flags strung from the yardarms to the corners of the patio. As befit a cottage named The Breakers, we had a house flag. Set against a white background, a black musical staff with four G notes represented the four Gullongs. Dad, who of course was the whole note, usually put them up in the morning while we kids were still asleep. The American flag went up first; then a navy union jack, signaling that we were firmly anchored at home, was raised on the left yardarm; and finally the house flag

Dad on flag duty.

to starboard. Taking them down was our job, including properly folding the American flag in triangles with the stars showing on the top.

"Time to take the flags down," said Dad. The sun was setting in a blaze to the west over Indiantown. The day was cooling off. Mom was yelling (softly) "Time to light the barbecue." All along the shoreline the smell of freshly burning lighter fluid mingled with the aroma of honeysuckle. Summer was in full swing.

Our barbecue was a rickety platform of tin, full of real charcoal. Dad stood over the grill in his bathing suit, brushing the chicken with barbecue sauce or turning the steak or the hamburgers. Dinner would be at the picnic table just outside the kitchen door.

Family friends would often drop in around dinnertime. This practice, virtually unheard of in the 21st century, was a welcome way of staying in touch in the 1950s. I remember longing to talk to Diane. Her phone in Wethersfield would ring and ring unanswered. Then a car would pull into the tiny grass driveway in back of the cottage facing the outdoor shower, and Diane and her parents *yoo-hooed* and *helloed* as they got out of the car. "We were just passing by and thought we'd say hello.

Lighting up the grill.

We were just taking a little drive down the shore." There seemed always to be "MIK"—more in the kitchen—more potato salad and more burgers to put on the grill.

The tides defined our days. Away from Cornfield Point for decades, I would dream of swimming there at high tide when the beach was sandy, the drop deep and quick, when you could get over your head in three steps and two strokes. At low tide we could walk to Town Beach along the packed, sand-waffled surface, crossing shallow pools of warm seawater filled with tiny crabs. Hieroglyphics of bird footprints and pieces of broken shells

Togetherness.

shimmered in the sunlight. In the distance we would see other walkers on the sandbar like space visitors, stick figures silhouetted as they ran and bent to pick up a shell or hold hands.

We swam at least twice a day every day and sat in the sun for hours. We were all bronzed and freckled. Sun block was something new, which we put on only in the very early spring. I can't remember Dad ever saying to me "I love you." But when he admired my tan and said, "You're all browned up," he might as well have. And as for his love of Mom, I remember one day as he looked out at her swimming in a bathing cap, her aquiline profile unsoftened by hair, saying "Doesn't she look beautiful?"

Dad commuted from Middletown in the summer. Arriving on a hot day, he would quickly change into his bathing suit and go for a swim. I liked to ride on his broad, brown back in the water. He would swim a few strokes of his strong crawl, then flip over onto his back and rest in the water, saying, "Ahhhh."

The cottage was headquarters for Dad's home-grown coast guard mission. Stationed on a chaise lounge, scanner radio tuned to marine air frequencies, he traced the horizon through field glasses. Radio Maydays brought high drama to an otherwise quiet afternoon. Every few weeks there was trouble right in front of our beach—a sailboat loose from its mooring, a swimmer in distress, a capsized boat—and Dad was out in the dinghy making a citizen rescue.

Fifty years later, doing some research for this story at the Saybrook Historical Society, I met Teddy, the Cornfield Point historian. When I told her my name, she said, "Oh, yes, your folks had The Breakers down by the beach." In fact, my folks, Dot and Bud Gullong, created this family life, made up this story, a postwar American dream. They both worked, Dad as a personnel manager at Raymond Engineering and Mom teaching Latin and French at Wethersfield High School. At the cottage they worked some more, Dad clearing the beach, mowing the lawn, and trimming the hedge, and Mom cooking, washing the windows, and making the beds with no cleaning lady, no dishwasher, and no washer-dryer.

They laughingly called it "togetherness." We were a happy family together at the cottage, swimming, playing hearts, and watching the glorious sunsets. But one of us was 13 and restless to know more about what was up on the other side of the hedge and on the other side of the horizon. A means of escape was near at hand. The good ship *Jan Bar*, a tiny speedboat was a few feet off our beach, secured to its mooring but ready to be unhooked for adventure.

Messing About in Boats

*Believe me, my young friend, there is nothing—
absolutely nothing—half so much worth doing
as simply messing about in boats. Simply
messing about in boats—or with boats. In or
out of 'em, it doesn't matter. Nothing seems to*

Launching my life in boating, Cornfield Point Beach, circa 1948.

*really matter, that's the charm of it. Whether
you get away, or whether you don't; whether
you arrive at your destination, or whether you
reach somewhere else, or whether you never
get anywhere at all, you're always busy, and
you never do anything in particular; and when
you've done it, there's always something else
to do, and you can do it if you like, but you'd
much better not.*

—Rat to Mole, rowing up a canal in Kenneth
    Grahame's *The Wind and the Willows*

It began with a sound—*rhoom, vroom, purr, hummm,*
the smell of gas, and the sight of a little churning whirl-
pool off the stern. The motor started after the third pull.
Idling on the mooring, I released its clip, pushed the
throttle, and sped towards the riptide chop off Cornfield
Point. I looked back to be sure that the little blue dinghy
was secured and rocking on the mooring. Mom was wav-
ing good-bye from the shore.

I was at the wheel of our little boat, the *Jan Bar,* well
before I learned to drive a car.

A 13-foot lapstrake, fiberglass boat with an 18-horse-
power motor, it was the craft that launched my lifetime
love of boats. Part nature, part nurture, boats were a family tradition.

Mom's grandfather Frederick Small was a genuine
Maine sea captain, his vessel plying the spice route from
the Carribean. Here is his daughter, our formidable Great

Great Aunt Betty.

Aunt Betty, setting sail with him for Martinique. The captain's telescope, a family treasure, sits in my brother's Cornfield Point house today.

Dad ran away to sea. That is how he told it at least. First, as a merchant marine, he saw Havana; then as a World War II naval ensign on the destroyer USS *Foote*, he saw action in the Pacific. But his first boat, like mine, was launched at Cornfield Point, Old Saybrook.

Below is Dad as a teenager in the stern of his canoe in front of the Cornfield Point bathing beach circa 1935. In the background is the cottage that 20 years later he would buy for our family.

Dad in his canoe.

With the *Jan Bar* ("Jane" and "Barton" truncated) full of friends, we could speed up the creeks (as we used to call the wetlands off Great Hammock Road), throwing our wake against the tall grass. We would fly past Half Tide Rock to Indiantown, entering its little harbor behind the breakwater. The people on the beach would watch us warily, intruders from another beach in an unknown craft piloted by children.

The grandest journey of independence was up the Connecticut River. Bouncing out of the Cornfield Point riptide, navigating well off the rocks, we would emerge into the calm along Knollwood Beach. The course was set for the Outer Light. We entered the river at the end of the breakwater—the very point where the first European explorer, Adrian Block, paused in 1614. We motored upriver and explored Hamburg Cove and Selden Creek. We entered Essex harbor, exalted at having made the trip on our own, only to look up to see the white Buick parked beside the steamboat dock in the cul- de-sac at the end of Main Street.

Mostly the *Jan Bar* stayed close to home. Without enough power for water skis, we pulled a surfboard. I got up on it once. After all, I had to run the boat. Mom would call us in for lunch or foul weather warnings by lowering the flags to half mast or blowing one long and two short on a whistle. We rowed home in the dingy called *Periwinkle,* dragged it over the rocks to the beach, and dreamed, as all boatowners do, of our next boat.

Luckily we had what Dad called "rich relatives." The

The *Jan Bar* crew ready for adventure.

Liebermans were into boating. We loved to walk past the "Owners Only" sign to visit them on the *Candy II* tied up at the Essex steamboat dock. There was no more elegant cabin cruiser on the Connecticut River than their 36-foot boat, built in the 1920s in Biddeford, Maine, and modernized in the 1950s. My cousin Leonard was the captain, navigating not by GPS but with a compass and charts. In boating, their world expanded and mine with it. There

The *Candy II.*

were boating friends from New York just back from the Bahamas. There were ropes, piles, fenders, and top-siders on our feet. There was a trip to Martha's Vineyard, where we were becalmed by a bell buoy in the fog then slipped into Oak Bluffs to eat fried clams and ride the merry-go-round.

My brother Bart was so hooked by our early boating life that he has never been without one. He went to Tabor Academy, where he rowed crew and trained on their tall ship, the *Tabor Boy,* and spent his Old Saybrook summers "in boating." He was the launch boy for the Essex Harbor Yacht Club, a lucrative job, rich in tips and probably apocryphal stories. My favorite involves a dog who barked from the deck of his boat for the launch to take him ashore for a meeting with a fire hydrant. You can't make this stuff up.

Bart then worked at The Ships' Store at the Terra Mar resort, where he sold boat gifts and equipment. He developed expertise in fiberglass rope and lighthouse ashtrays. And he made and shared with me many new boating friends—with the Seligsons, the Segeloffs, and the Beckensteins, we, too, were in boating.

The *Jan Bar* was followed for Bart with swift, air-conditioned Searays and Aquasports. Dad ended his boating life in style as a deckhand and guide for the Deep River Steamship Company. Posing as an old salt, he told tourists stories of shad in the river, rum running in the sound, and riding out the hurricane of 1938 at the Castle. Leonard Lieberman, the *Candy II* captain, turned

Zerlina.

to sailing with his family, but as he approached the age of 80, he told me that "in boating now I prefer to go as Commodore."

As for me, in 1994 I was almost 50 when a dreamboat tied up at the Dock and Dine. It was Robert Brown in his Sea Dory named *Zerlina*. With Robert and *Zerlina* as my new companions, I was in boating again.

But first I had to grow up.

Robert Brown on *Zerlina*, charting our course.

The Lazy, Hazy, Crazy Days of Summer

In the summer of 1958 at the tender age of 13, I entered for the first time that Valhalla of teenage culture called hanging out. Nothing in the grown-up world compares to teenage hanging out. No bars or clubs are needed. All that is required is the gathering of three or more teens wherever parents are out of sight. I began hanging out right outside our cottage on West Shore Drive on the road that ran atop the Cornfield Point Association Beach. I could preview the action from my bedroom window.

We were a fluid community, ranging in age from 13 to 21, easy to join just by walking up and saying "hi." Some kids were around for just one night or one week, but the hard core kids like me were out walking by 7:00 or 7:30 most evenings of the summer. We didn't drink. We had never heard of marijuana. No one smoked. Our main interests were one another.

Curly-haired, tanned, freckled Billy Patterson led the pack with charm. The first night he put his arm around me, I recorded the triumph in my diary. I dreamed he would talk to me again the next night. "When are we going out to dinner?" he crooned. He couldn't afford to buy me ice cream, let alone dinner. But girls could dream.

And that is what I did most of the first summer of hanging out, singing the Everly Brothers' hit "All I Have to Do is Dream": "I can make you mine/kiss your lips of wine/any time night or day."

Coming and going formed the narrative of our evenings. As a 14-year-old diarist, I reported what happened one day in 1959:

> *Thursday night was a ball. Don and Frankie were pretending to smoke cigars. Billy came up behind me and poked my waist. Larry kept patting my head. A good night! Later Don, Frankie, Sue, and I went over to Jan's house. Today the girls came over to get me, and we went to the beach. Sue, Jan, Carol, and I talked to Zohn until Bill, Joan, Linda, Larry, and Don came over. Bill landed next to me. Later Carol went for a walk with Breen somebody. Sue and I kept talking to Frankie and Zohn. Then Linda and Joan came. Then Carol and Breen came. Breen did a lot of talking to me.*

Cars came by from parts unknown, driven by boys from other beaches like Chalker or Indiantown or the honky-tonk place across the river, Sound View. Most of us just stared at these slick and possibly dangerous men of the world, old enough to have licenses and cars. In the film they would all be played by James Dean. Suzanne, who was tough and fearless herself, usually greeted them. One night she walked up to the car door and leaned in close to talk to a boy called Pennsylvania, a passenger in a blue Plymouth Fury. Ten minutes later, he was killed drag racing, the Fury wrapped around a tree on Maple Avenue. We went to the wake, a group of teenage girls, briefly mourning a boy we didn't know and never would.

But mostly we had fun. We gathered always on the third farthest section of the beach and spread our blankets near each other. Boys were buried in the sand by groups of girls. Groups of boys threw screaming girls wishing and hoping to be chosen into the water.

Hanging out at Cornfield Point Beach, circa 1959.

Beach girls.

Every Sunday night there were movies on the beach—
families gathered on their blankets in the front and teens
in the back. Billy Patterson landed on my blanket. Sigh.
There were parties. We actually played spin the bottle
and yes, there I received the official first kiss. The diarist
sums up the social scene:

> I danced as much as everyone else. I think
> I like Frankie Budarz. The party was just
> dreamy. It was under Carol's willow tree. She
> had a big bonfire for toasting marshmallows,
> and the moon was full. We drank soda, and it
> looked just like a Coke advertisement.

That first summer on the beach, I launched the lifelong process of sizing myself up. I wonder in the diary
how a senior could like a freshman who "looks like me." I
fear that there will be necking at a party and am sure no
one wants to neck with me.

I make a to-do list of categories for self-improvement, guidelines such as good study habits, handwriting, appearance (the longest), and finally, charm:

    a. Speak to everyone who's name you know.

    b. Make other people feel important.

    c. Never talk about yourself, always the other
       person.

Bathing suits, the uniform of the day, inspired many opportunities for self loathing. I was fat. I was pimply and hairy. I had just finished a delicious breakfast of bacon, eggs, toast, and two pieces of coffee cake. I felt guilty. Still, I had one perfect bathing suit, golden and saronged in the center for slimming, with strong round cups that I left half empty.

The Swimsuit Issue. I am second from right.

By the summer of 1961 I had met Peter Bride. We sat on the beach and talked under the moon. We swam to the raft, took off our bathing suits, and he reached for me as I swam to shore. We lay down on a towel, lifted our heads, looked towards the sea wall as the skunk walked by. The loveliest boy at Cornfield Point and I had never even kissed.

The lazy, hazy days of summer also infected Mom and Dad. In her old age, Mom remembered having sex at the cottage. I knew it! Instead of the scolding and scheduling of real life, they led us on adventures. Dad would drive by in his Chevy convertible (successor to the Buick) and pile my group of teens into the car for a trip to Johnny Ad's or for a Lamplighter special: a double burger with bacon and special sauce.

Mom provided culture. She took me to the movies in Essex and Old Saybrook. We saw *Kings Go Forth* with Natalie Wood, Bing Crosby, and Tony Curtis and *Reluctant Debutante* with Sandra Dee. Thrillingly we went to the theater. At the Ivoryton Playhouse my favorite television stars, mostly single women with jobs, leapt from the screen and were right there on that tiny stage. We waited at the stage door to get Betsy Palmer's autograph and somehow got to greet Susie MacNamara, the "Private Secretary," aka Ann Sothern, backstage.

But most of all, Mom took me shopping. From the Outdoor Trader in Essex and Thurston's in Old Saybrook, we assembled the perfect outfit for Saturday nights: black bermudas, a pink check shirt, a Shetland cardigan, and a green belt. A shopping trip to Bradlee's in New London netted a tan, orlon slip-on sweater, a trench coat, and a red bouffant petticoat (to go under the poodle skirt I already had)—the total cost coming in under the budget of $15.

In 1995 Mom, in her 80s, came back to live with me in Old Saybrook. We could still shop at Thurston's. She moved slowly as she tried on her favorite polyester pant suits, while I remembered her 50 years before, standing outside a dressing room smiling encouragement as I struggled into a possible new bathing suit. The diary captured the romance:

> *I love summer. We have such a ball. Riding around in Jan's car. Walking. Going over to someone's house. Standing and talking. Swimming. Lying on the beach. The beginning of this week brought nothing too exciting except for the fact that I was here . . . which is pretty good in itself. I love this house and beach so much. The air is so cool, free, and fresh here, and the sound of the waves is an endless lullaby. We're awfully lucky to have this place. I'm sure it's the loveliest spot on Long Island Sound.*

These lazy, hazy, crazy days were unfolding all along the Connecticut shore in the little cottage communities. But by the summer of 1965, I was bored.

Get A Job

As my 15th birthday approached, hanging out was no longer enough for me. I wanted to engage with the wider world. I wanted to work. Summer jobs were an internship in the adult world.

It began on Cornfield Point, where I went to work as a day camp counselor for the beach association. On rainy days we wove potholders on tiny hand looms in the clubhouse. In the sunshine I taught little children to swim, to float, and to dog paddle. "Take a breath and blow bubbles," I chanted. At the end of the first week, I had a Social Security number and a check for $2.50.

The big money was in babysitting. Guilty parents would pay far above the $1.00 per hour minimum wage, especially if they had been out drinking at the Castle. I built a robust client base by leafleting the mailboxes along the little lanes of Cornfield Point.

I pursued job training in collaboration with my mother. She ferried me in the Buick to Valley Regional High School, where I learned to type on a large black

Underwood typewriter with an inky black ribbon. She took me to early morning classes in Red Cross water safety instruction at Clinton Town Beach. There I weathered mouth-to-mouth, the fireman's carry, strenuous lap crawls, and earned my lifeguard certification. Now, on the one hand, thanks to continuing education, I was equipped to be a girl Friday; and on the other, thanks to the Red Cross, to sit in the sun by a pool all day.

The Terra Mar was impressed with my Red Cross certification, and I was hired. I never did see Frank Sinatra in the pool, despite stories of Rat Pack visits to the resort. Not only was I a lifeguard, but I also joined a synchronized swim group inspired by Esther Williams and the modernist fantasies of Terra Mar's three circular pools. By

The 1950s modern swimming pool, Terra Mar, Old Saybrook. (Saybrook Point Inn photo)

the August performance, I had missed so many practices that I was kicked poolside by the coach, dressed in a grass skirt, and ordered to scatter flowers onto the water during the performance. Sorry that Frank had to miss that.

It soon became clear that my real calling was in hospitality. I belonged in the restaurant business. I started behind the soda fountain counter at Doane's Pharmacy in Centerbrook. There I learned product management, i.e. the exact size of a scoop of ice cream, and developed the muscles in my right arm. The customers at this bar were sober and often sad, telling me tales of loss—divorce and joblessness, craziness, and old age. I was a lucky young girl, listening and pouring their milk shakes, in a uniform my mother had ironed.

Customers at my next gig, The Terra Mar Snack Bar, were a happier lot. Fresh off their yachts, they talked about racing, bluefish, and the price of gas. Loss was not for them. I was taken under the wing of a beautiful movie starlet of a girl named Elaine Stella. She presided over the staff house across the street, where most of my colleagues were spending the summer in sexual mayhem and bliss. I turned my young attention eagerly to Elaine's tales of a world I was still far from entering.

Soon I got out from behind the counters and into the dining room of The Dock & Dine. Serving was a real profession at this legendary Old Saybrook restaurant overlooking the Connecticut River. Waitresses were responsible for the check in each party. I would indicate each price, add it up, and make the change almost always

Me, waitressing at the Terra Mar Snack Bar, circa 1960.

in cash. If a server made a mistake, it was deducted from his or her wages. Various forms of upselling increased the check averages and, of course, the tips. The most famous and successful waitress, Annie, would sell as many as 30 bottles of wine on good nights. She was swift and skillful with the corkscrew.

My personal techniques leaned to "local girl" and "college girl" earning money for education. We worked in teams. Luckily I was paired with Brian, a swift-of-foot, working-class British boy on a temporary work visa. He could manage the emotions in the kitchen and move food and set-ups out fast, leaving me in charge of the money and working the floor with youthful charm. Brian called me "lovey" as we closed out each night, splitting the tips.

Like most restaurants, the Dock & Dine was pure theater. In the lobby at the door was Mr. Lovell, the grand old man of down-the-river restaurants, a former owner of the Griswold Inn. Backstage, the kitchen was a hot, chaotic oven, alive with mumbling in Spanish, screams of "pick-up," "86," and clanging dishes. In the orchestra of the dining room, customers drank Tom Collins and ate clams, lobsters, and baked potatoes with sour cream.

Presiding over all were Steffie and Eddie Walters, Austrian immigrants who created a shoreline landmark beloved more for location than cuisine, the destination of so many drives down the shore. As my summer there ended, Mrs. Walters took my hand and said "I'm glad you came with us this summer . . . you nice girl."

It would take my next job—at the Castle—to lead the nice girl into temptation.

The Castle Inn:
A Romance

L ast night I dreamed that I was at the Castle again. It was the summer of 1964. A virgin not yet 18 without prospects of love or employment, I went up the Billow Road hill towards the Castle on Cornfield Point on the bluff overlooking Long Island Sound.

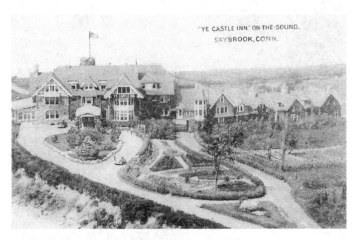

An early postcard of the Castle. (Old Saybrook Historical Society photo)

All I knew of romance was gothic. Daphne de Maurier's *Rebecca*, Charlotte Brönte's *Jane Eyre*. This castle in Cornfield Point could have been Manderley. It could have been Thornfield Hall.

I walked from the lower parking lot up three stone steps to the high road and followed it to the circular drive under the portico. I opened the door into a grand entry hall. Beside the massive stone fireplace stood a rather ugly, dark, little man. He looked deeply into my eyes, reached out his hand to mine and said "Do you want a summer job, cookie?" Mr. Rochester, I presume.

The Castle seen from Long Island Sound still marks Cornfield Point. Now a private home, it has returned to its origins, built in 1905 as the estate of George Jarvis Beach. By 1920 it was proposed to anchor the development of

Dancing at the Castle with Dad.

Cornfield Point as the association's club. By 1924 Ye Olde Castle Inn opened, beginning its decades-long run as a restaurant, hotel, and setting for stories.

The Castle and its history seemed to belong to all of us. It was a place for celebrations. The dining rooms overlooked Long Island Sound. There was a dance floor and the coziest little cocktail lounge, a true boite. My parents might "slip away" for a drink at the Castle. Friends got married there. I celebrated my college graduation there and danced with my father.

We were always talking about the fate of the Castle. Who owned it? How was the food? Were they busy? Were there any movie stars staying there? Was it for sale? Would it close after the summer?

There were so many stories. Dad rode out the hurricane of 1938 at the Castle, safe from the murderous storm, which killed hundreds of people throughout New England. The estate turned into an army munitions testing center; the glory days of gambling and rum running when the Lindberghs ran it under prohibition; the German waiters who went home to fight for Hitler; actors from the Ivoryton Playhouse who slept there.

But I had a story of my own. It was not a dark and stormy night when I met Gene Kowalski, one of the brothers who bought the Castle in 1963. They opened it for their first summer in 1964. But there might well have been ominous portents of my first few weeks of work. "We have to get the place ready to open, so I want you to work for my sister, who is going to be our head housekeeper," said Gene, gleaming with anticipation of the busy summer season ahead.

I learned to make beds and clean toilets for the first time in my formerly pampered life. Gene would come by to eye the plumbing and often turn a similarly inspective glance towards me. He was one of the first touchy-feely men I had ever met. He would put an arm around my aching shoulder, which had just scrubbed six johns, sinks, and tubs.

"I am working as a wombat," I exclaimed to my parents. This lament of the spoiled (in this case, me) stood not for the cuddly Australian creature but "Waste Of Money, Brains, And Talent." Surely I could prepare for college better by studying for SATs on the beach.

So then I quit. I found Gene in the dining room and very apologetically said that I was just not suited for this job. "Well, sweetie," he said soulfully, "I just can't let you go. We'll just have to find something else for you to do. Come back in on Tuesday. I have some ideas." He couldn't let me go? I felt as thrilled as if I had just been embraced. I thought about the Castle and its owner all weekend.

Gene was full of ideas. He was redecorating everywhere with drapes and statues and Orientalia. He was planning advertising and special events. Not only did toilets have to be kissing sweet, the guests had to be welcomed and coddled. I knew nothing about the Kowalski brothers except that they (Gene, Leon, and Henry) were from New Jersey. I never knew if they had run hotels or restaurants before or what set them on this adventure.

But looking back on it with the perspective of 50 years, it is clear that they were amateurs with a big dream and Gene was the lead fabulist, the creator of the magic.

Had I not been so thrilled, I might have known that these guys really didn't know what they were doing when Gene suggested that I become the hostess and social director of the Castle. As a girl addicted to Gale Storm's 1950s TV show *Oh! Susanna,* in which she plays a social director on a cruise ship, I thought that being social director seemed the perfect path to a fabulous summer with pay. The job description was vague, and my experience in all aspects of it was nonexistent. In other words I fit in perfectly with the management team's business plan.

I wrote ads by the seat of my pants, got the brothers' approval, and placed them in the *New York Times* and *New London Day.* I set up destination lunches—wine tastings, fashion shows, and hair-style demonstrations. I greeted guests, took their complaints and comments, served bouillon at the pool in the mornings and tea in the afternoon. As we got busier, I was called upon more and more to waitress, which involved serving cocktails— or not. Gene said "Sweetie, you just had a birthday."

Through it all I fell in love with Gene. "How can I feel so close to this ugly little man?" I asked myself in my diary. But that was it—he was a man, not a college boy. Gene had a romantic personality. Creative, imaginative, dreaming, warm, and flirtatious, he connected with me, he connected with the single female guests, and there was no wife in sight. Mrs. Kowalski was not locked up in the attic but was somewhere in New Jersey seeking a divorce, no doubt mentioning promises unfulfilled and roving attentions.

My Mr. Rochester, I mean, Gene, was sensitive, lonely, an artist. He was a man of the world—short, but to me he had inner stature. And there he was in the fieldstone Castle on a cliff above the sea.

One quiet day at the Castle he said, "Come on upstairs, I want to sketch you." Fear and excitement coursed through my body. I was wearing a skirt and jersey. He

Portrait of the Author as a Young Girl.

posed me on a bed and talked and drew. "You have a nice figure for an old lady." He moved me to another pose. He looked at me. There it was for the first time in my virginal life—the male gaze—and I welcomed it with my whole, young, romantic heart. As he finished sketching, he handed me the drawings and said "Next time I want you to pose nude."

Reader, I did not marry him. Nor did I ever take my clothes off at the Castle. I will never know if Gene was seriously considering seducing me or if it was just a teasing turn of phrase. Reality entered romance in the form of chaos in the kitchen, at the switchboard, and in the cocktail lounge. Guests wanted lox and bagels at breakfast, and Henry drove to New Haven to buy them. Customers demanding lobsters meant someone had to run to Abbott's in Noank to bring them back. Walter Pigeon, direct from the Ivoryton Playhouse, arrived trailing Hollywood entitlement and screaming in fury about the lack of room service. Alone at the front desk switchboard, I pretended to transfer him to the restaurant and watch later as he stomped out of the Castle, destination unknown.

The staff, working people who needed serious, permanent jobs, came and went. The cocktail lounge naturally seemed to be the most successful part of the business with a piano man named Walter Kelly Pegeen, a singer, and a busy bartender named Sam. I filled in everywhere—at the reservation desk and in the dining room. The Castle's short-staffed waitresses put together their own appetizers and desserts in the kitchen, bused the tables, and served the drinks. Shrimp cocktails were made by putting ice in a glass, hooking on six shrimp, and making a side of cocktail sauce. Clams on the half shell had to be opened. Salads set up. Crème de menthe parfaits were scooped and poured and whip-creamed by the waitstaff. One night we served 300 guests while the always angry chef never showed up.

Doom was gathering over the turrets of the Castle. An elderly distinguished man named Roy Brown appeared one day. He prowled the grounds and set up an office, apparently having purchased the Castle with plans to turn the site of leisure and escape into a citadel of learning for young boys.

And then there was Patti, the new cocktail waitress. Suddenly Gene grew cool and treated me like just one of the employees. My exhaustion with the hours and the pay increased as the sexual harassment (which now it surely would be deemed) ceased. One night I hid behind a hedge to watch them walking hand in hand. I knew that the end of my romance was in sight.

Gene's sons, whose summer jobs involved dishwashing in the Castle kitchen, sealed the end one evening when I overheard them discussing Patti. "I like her!" said one. "Sure," replied the other, "but do you know what she is and what a deal she has shacked up with our old man and still earning a fat salary? While we are in here, breaking our backs."

And so I quit again, this time for good. I avoided Gene and handed in my apron to his brother Henry. I told him I was sad and grateful for the opportunity to have been part of their plans but that I had to (white lie) go to summer school.

In truth, I had to go—to Europe, to college, to Boston, to New York. The time to leave Old Saybrook for the first time had arrived.

She's Leaving Home

It is now the summer of 1968, and the political is personal is political. The four-Gs flag is still flying over The Breakers, but we are a family in transition, each facing change and moving to another stage of our lives.

Sooner or later children will break your heart. In the summer of 1968 at Cornfield Point, I was the prodigal betrayer, plotting my escape, thanklessly self-involved. Aged 23 and obsessed with sex and money, I had access to neither at home. I was trying to figure out how to launch my life after a year of graduate school at the Boston University School of Public Communications. I had graduated from Connecticut College, made two trips to Europe, and was living on the Connecticut shore without student loan debt, without rent payments, and without ever having cooked a meal. I was a pre-adult, longing to leave the daddy and mother who had sacrificed and invested so much in me.

"She's leaving home after all these years/we gave her everything money could buy/bye-bye," as the Beatles sang.

Without exception my parents disliked my boy-friends. Nice Jewish boys. Irish charmers. Waspy graduates of Princeton or Harvard. There were no exceptions. I couldn't figure it out until now, looking back. None of them were good enough for me. They were right.

Richard Gross was the first detestable. My father once called him a long-haired bastard. A reporter with United Press International in Boston, Richard visited Cornfield Point. To my parents he was a visitor from another planet, planet New York, where he grew up in the Bronx. To me he was a friend with a gentle kindness only I could see—full of curiosity and energy. He talked to my parents. He bought them a thoughtful house gift, a black whale paperweight for my father, who loved whales. What was it they did not like about him? My mother said "You don't have to take the first one who comes along."

As always, the weather at Cornfield Point was a backdrop to our emotional dramas.

Frequent thunderstorms raged outside my window overlooking the beach. Rain banged on the windows. The surf pounded. The house seemed to shake. The sky blazed. The waves came steadily, crashing, waiting. And I was reading *Lady Chatterly's Lover*. Seriously.

We were gathered at the cottage, the center of our family happiness, each of us in some personal turmoil and misery. My parents were nearing 60, their careers winding down and their children moving on.

My father was ready to retire, frustrated by the marketing hotshots and MBAs who had joined his growing

Surf crashing in front of The Breakers, Cornfield Point.

company, Raymond Engineering. Dad was director of personnel and head security officer responsible for an array of government contracts as Raymond became a leading Connecticut military and aerospace manufacturer. He had slipped into management from the worker side and suffered from taking responsibility too seriously. He took early retirement soon after the summer of 1968.

In the summer of 1968, my mother was between terms teaching at the Long Lane School, a reform school in Middletown, Connecticut. She had migrated to Long Lane after a long and committed career as a high school teacher. After having two children in 1945 and 1948, she returned to teaching at Wethersfield High School. She taught French, English, and Latin, but it was Latin for which she was renowned, thanks to the annual Roman banquets she threw in the gym for her students—toga-clad, reclining decliners—*amo, amas, amat.*

Like my father, Mom fell afoul of administration and its new requirements for commitments outside the classroom, which she had always made willingly. One study hall assignment over the line caused her to stand her ground and quit with the local newspaper trumpeting "Veteran Teacher Quits in Labor Dispute."

The catch was that she needed to teach for three more years to qualify for her much-deserved pension. It turned out that Long Lane was a sort of paradise for education in which discipline was provided by the guards and matrons and lessons were given by the teachers. In the last years of her teaching career, my mother had new and close encounters with students from troubled urban settings, like the ones erupting in turmoil in Chicago and Los Angeles in 1968.

In the summer of 1968, my parents, each in their own ways, were changing perhaps as much as I was. Inside the family there was a perfect storm of change just as there was in the nation as a whole. The steady, hard-working paths of their mid-lives were coming to a close while I was trying to set out on mine. We were at an impasse, filled with anger and tears. Now, when I read in my diary "Mom was crying," I can hardly bear the shame and guilt I feel at having made my mother cry.

It is hard to remember or even know what was wrong between my parents and me. In many ways I was a model daughter. I had done well in college and continued to work in the summers, commuting to the Connecticut College News Office in New London where I wrote press releases about the dance festival and "home towns" about students.

Work and friendships were going well. Standing on our beach, I opened the *New London Day*, August 19, 1967, to the two-page spread I had written on Amala Shankar, an Indian dance teacher at the Connecticut College Festival. The *Day* had used my press release word for word. My friends loved my parents and loved to visit the cottage. Mom made fish chowder for Debbie White's wedding party.

My parents had invented the wonderful family life we shared at Cornfield Point. But when I was there, I regressed. Away in Boston I found an apartment on Marlborough Street and drank scotch. I moved to New York and lived in Greenwich Village. I was free for friendships, work, love affairs, and for my own mistakes. At the cottage I feared falling back into childhood, losing my new self. "I was a woman," I wrote in my diary and "there I feel like a blowfish."

I was outgrowing my parents, or trying to. They perhaps were just mourning the emptying nest and the ending of the family summers of togetherness.

We started to say good-bye together. I listed farewells in my diary, "looking out the window and feeling this air, a sail with Peter Kahn, a cigarette with Suzanne, a conversation with Ginny, a cheeseburger on the picnic table, the voices outside on the beach, sitting on the patio in the chaise in the sun."

All adults now, we went to dinner together at the Castle. I wrote "Sitting in the Castle, it stormed a chiarschuro, and the rain moved on and off the shore, and it was warm and pink glowing inside, and the place was full of memories for me—ghosts—memories moving warmly through me as we talked and I sipped the Tia Maria ..."

We discussed our shared fantasy, one held by so many Old Saybrook residents and visitors, that one day we would buy the Castle. The Castle served its last meal, checked out its last guest more than 20 years ago. The real estate was worth more than the hospitality but not worth more than the memories.

Mom and Dad sold our cottage in 1969. Soon it was torn down and replaced with a huge modern house that towered over the hedge.

Dot and Bud retired. They left not only Cornfield Point but Wethersfield behind and moved permanently to 512 Maple Avenue in Fenwood. Now I could say without hesitation that I was from Old Saybrook. My parents lived there and from time to time I visited them.

Maple Avenue

I moved to New York on the night of the first moon landing, July 16, 1969. Old Saybrook might as well have been the moon for me for the next few years. It was far away from the action of my life. Mom and Dad were there on Maple Avenue, enjoying their retirement. They had a new set of neighborhood friends—the Dobbs, the Lonergans, and others—and at last they traveled to Greece, Rome, Vienna, and to Florida every winter.

Richard Gross had left me for a job in Israel. Mom and Dad were right. Packy McGinnis was my new love, a real New Yorker and an executive at Lincoln Center where I was working. He took me to his childhood home on Staten Island. I took him to Cornfield Point. We stayed at the Mohegan Hotel in New London, drove to Old Saybrook, and sneaked onto the rock in front of our old cottage. Once again, the metaphorical surf was pounding.

Finally I told my parents that Packy and I were living together on 96th Street and unlikely to get married in the near future. He was getting a divorce. Now they had real reasons for distress. But times were changing, they were getting older, and they tried rapprochement. We were invited to visit. There were two guest rooms in the Maple Avenue ranch house, where Packy and I dutifully slept separately. He was so charming and friendly. How could they not love him as I did? Unmoved, my father called him "Songs, Dances, and Funny Stories."

Not to be outdone, Dad proposed to entertain our New York friends with a grand New England tradition: a shad bake. Packy, whose father had once been president of the New Haven Railroad, insisted we book the first-class car. I procured souvenir fish charms made of silver in Times Square and etched them with Shad Bake, May 15, 1977. There was no end to our creativity.

The party was a chimera, a vision of the possibility that we could share our lives as friends. Aunt Katie, cousin Peggy, and a couple kids from the next generation of Liebermans were there. Leonard's son Peter helped to build the huge, blazing fire. The New York friends were suitably representative—the regional theater actress Esther Benson; Delmar Hendricks, who managed the Lincoln Center theaters; our new friend Celeste, who looked like all my gym teachers but really was a lesbian; Joan Spivak, whom I met in consciousness raising; Tina Ramirez, who was starting Ballet Hispanico, soon to be a renown national dance company; Larry Nicks, who dealt commercial real estate between acting jobs. We played croquet and badminton and walked the beach while waiting for the feast.

Dad pushing smoke towards the planked Connecticut River shad.

Dad planked the shad—that is, he nailed fillets to boards and angled them in back of the fire. The shad roasted in the smoke, the heat melting the fish's famous bones. On the barbecue Mom sautéed the roe in butter. This was one of the happiest days of my life.

One of the worst was on Maple Avenue after a long Thanksgiving dinner with the Liebermans in Chester. Their grandchildren were growing up. One rose after grace to announce his engagement to the stunned family. Everybody but Aunt Katie had started to drink, and the scotch was flowing along with the pumpkin and minced meat pies. Back at Maple Avenue we stood around the kitchen on our way to bed. Packy to my father: "I want to sleep with your daughter tonight." If my heart hadn't been breaking, it could have been a sitcom scene. Slug. Crumple. Shuffle. Dad punched my boyfriend. He fell back against the wall and started to slide down. Dad stormed out of the kitchen, leaving Packy alive. We went each to our own beds, me sobbing and he passing out. Smaller than Dad, Packy followed him around the house, down to the basement, into the yard all the next morning apologizing, but to no avail.

Back in New York, back on the moon, my parents and I were estranged for a year or so. Packy, our many friends, and I led a merry chase of work and love. But as the years rolled on, it was clear that he, too, was leaving me for a powerful rival. Packy was becoming a drunk, leaving me for vodka. My parents were right again.

I began to visit them on my own in Old Saybrook, and we had lovely times—dinners at the Dock & Dine, Luigi's, or at Dad's favorite, Mr. T's. The judgments and the angers were gone. I was an adult living somewhere on the moon. Dad and I sat up on the porch, with its sliver view of the sound, after everyone else had gone to bed, and we talked. Mostly it was small talk about the neighbors or my job. It was not so important what was said but that we were talking. In the background we could hear the waves and the traffic on Maple Avenue. Then he, too, was gone.

Calling from the hospital, Bart reached me at a party

for the Public Theater, where I worked in New York. He insisted I needed to get in a cab and come to Middletown immediately—to the hospital where we were both born. "This cannot be happening," I said to myself over and over again during the long cab ride. "Bart is overreacting, dramatizing." Greeting us in the waiting room, the doctor said, "Your father is dying." We spent the night there, not sleeping—going in and out of his room to say goodbye.

"How are you doing?" I asked him. "Poorly," he replied. "We love you," Mom said, and I always wondered if, when alone with him that night, she had said "I." Bart said to Dad, "Barbara and I are going to get married and have children, and so you would have grandchildren after all." I said nothing.

The breezeway doors to the house on Maple Avenue opened and closed all day. The Fenwood neighbors took over the kitchen. Old family friends walked in the door. The Aherns, the Dahlbergs, the Stevens. Bobby Beckenstein walked in with a giant platter of sandwiches, which is all we ate for the next week. The phone rang constantly. Calls from New York friends, murmuring comfort. Fitfully sleeping, I woke up and remembered that it was still true. Here, for the first time in my life, was grief.

Mother was 77. Dad, her Bud, her buddy, was dead at 74. I went often to Old Saybrook for the rest of the summer of 1986. She cried and cried. So did I. She said, "Life is not worth living without him. I just want to join Bud." But this was the woman who left Mars Hill, Maine, alone in 1939 to teach in Connecticut. By the next summer she was ready to go on. 512 Maple Avenue was on the market, and she had found a condo in Naples, Florida. "What about your old friends?" I asked. "What will you do for friends in Florida?" "I'll make new ones," she replied.

The yard sale was the last stage of grief, a letting go and saying farewell to family life. My childhood toy chest, the Fafnir meat grinder, vases, bowls, and linen napkins went. Lobster buoys, garage tools, ropes, and hoses were carried off for a song by the early birds.

The moving day was scheduled, but there was still time for one last laugh. Mom told us she got a phone call from the buyer of her home, asking permission to bury her dad in the Maple Avenue back garden before the closing. Bart called the future owner of 512 Maple Avenue and discovered that she actually wanted to bury her beloved dog, not her father, at her new Old Saybrook home. Mom, going a little deaf, left soon thereafter for Florida.

I was also trying to move on. The patriarch and the interloper boyfriend were both gone, their rivalry ending in a sad draw. By August 1987 my mother and I— alone on Maple Avenue, she aged 78 and I at 42—were both done with Old Saybrook. I wrote in my diary, "What am I doing here, where there are no artists, no restaurants, and no theaters? I have driven around alone in my father's Chevy convertible as if I were Maria in (Joan Didion's) *Play It As It Lays*. Only I am not in L.A.—not suicidal—just anxious."

Seven or so years passed without a Gullong in Old Saybrook. Bart lived on Long Island and I in New York with yet another boyfriend. Neil Chrisman and I got off I-95 once in Old Saybrook to buy liquor. Unless I knew someone in Fenwick, he didn't even want to drive down to the river. We were on our way to Martha's Vineyard, where Princeton alumnae were more highly represented in the summer population. Mom, of course, disapproved, and in time he left me for a more socially appropriate partner.

I visited Mom in Naples, Florida, every two months. She was happy there, playing bridge and enjoying many new friends. But summers were brutal. Once I had left Martha's Vineyard, I too needed a summer respite. By the spring of 1993, we both were dreaming of Old Saybrook again. We rented a ranch-house cottage set on a slab of concrete jutting into Long Island Sound on Cornfield Point a few houses up West Shore Drive from the former site of The Breakers.

It was a homecoming for us both. I was temporarily the mistress of this house set so familiarly on Cornfield Point facing the sound and the sunsets. It seemed to me the prow of a ship where I, the confident pilot, am feeling good about myself as I approach 50 with my 84-year-old mother by my side. "A mitzvah," my friend Karen calls it.

We were back. Mom was reunited with friends and family. Elinor Sanstrom and Kay Giannotta were around every other day for lunches at the Hide-Away. Aunt Katie was nearing 90 and fragile, but Peggy arranged frequent visits, wrapping her in a blanket in a chair on Cornfield Point near where 70 years before she had sat cross-legged on the beach. I walked down Town Beach Road to buy the *New York Times* at the corner beach store, remembering the 15-year-old who more than 30 years before walked this street to leave her babysitting flyers in the mailboxes.

In New York I was working for an international cultural exchange agency, making new friends from around the world. What better model for an American town is there than Old Saybrook? Ana Maria Palma, a gorgeous Chilean actress and diplomat, swam off the rocks and then cooked gambas for us. We took Edith Markson, the doyenne of Russian theater exchange to a church supper in Chester. Sydney Selepe visited from Soweto, South

Returning to Cornfield Point: Mom, Aunt Katie, cousin Peggy, Bart and Linda Gullong.

Africa. Mom served them crab rolls and New England fish chowder. Here's her recipe:

Fish Chowder

Render tiny bits of salt pork, plus one large piece, in a frying pan.

Cook onions in the rendered pork until translucent.

Separately cover and cook the haddock in water.

Flake and skin the fish.

Add fish water to the onion mixture and add thinly sliced potatoes.

Cook until tender, adding lots of salt and pepper.

Add the fish to the onions and potatoes.

Scald and add milk.

Serve with saltines and pickles.

Between visitors at our rental, I rode my bike and grabbed some local headlines. At last the path along the causeway from Fenwick to Terra Mar had been widened. No longer would bikers have to share the death-defyingly narrow road with automobile traffic. Alas, however, it turned out that the only way to get a bike onto the path was to lift it over the aluminum guard rail that extended right across the entrance. What is a New York girl to do but call the press? The *Shoreline Times* and I staged the photo below. The state department of transportation removed the barrier. Next time I will pose without the helmet.

As the summer neared its close, Mom and I met with Bea Fitzgerald. We were looking for real estate again. This time the Gullong house in Old Saybrook would be mine.

Photo by Robert MacDonnell

Jane Gullong enjoys bike riding, but lifting her bicycle over the railing on the Fenwick side of the Fenwick Causeway to get onto the main road is no sport.

Safety improvements shortchange cyclists

■ IN BRIEF: The "new and improved" Fenwick Causeway allows east access to the pedestrian and bikeway only from the Old Saybrook side, not from Fenwick.

By Vallerie A. Malkin
Staff Writer

OLD SAYBROOK - The improvements to the Fenwick Causeway connecting the borough of Fenwick to the town of Old Saybrook may look nice, but local bikers are wondering why a path created for pedestrians, fishermen and bikers fails to accommodate the latter.

The pedestrian and bike pathway was widened and a safety railing installed, permitting bicyclists, pedestrians and fishermen to access the pier without endangering them to traffic. But there is no exit path from the walkway to the main road on the Fenwick side, so bicyclists are forced to lift their bikes over the railing.

a big strong guy, lifting a bike over, and (the railing) is too high to do it easily."

Officials at the Department of Transportation (DOT) said they are aware of the problem. "We are going to do something to change it," said Robert Fisher, the project engineer for the Fenwick Causeway.

Gullong contacted Fisher at the DOT to ask him if anything was going to be done.

"He was very helpful and nice," said Gullong of Fisher. Fisher said there is nothing to be done to change the current design, and that a new contract

would have to be issued to open up the railing about five feet, similar to what appears on the Old Saybrook side.

The difficulty, according to Fisher, is finding someone to fabricate a new railing in a short period of time, because it usually takes between five and six months. By then, biking season will be over.

"We are looking for someone to do it quicker," said Fisher. Construction began on the causeway in September and was completed by Brunalli Construction of Southington on July 1.

From the *Shoreline Times*.

23 Neptune Drive

It was not my dream house. A two-bedroom ranch—tiny rooms on a tiny lot in Knollwood with stunning views of the neighbors—became my weekend retreat in the spring of 1994. I also hadn't dreamed that, as I neared my 50th birthday, I would be sharing a house with my mother. I had seen *Grey Gardens*. At least when Edie Beale found herself living with her mother, they were in the Hamptons. Mom and I both determined to make the best of it in Knollwood, and we more than did.

In my studio apartment in New York City, I longed for a nearby beach, a garden, lots of closet space, and kitchen cabinets full of pots and pans. In her condo in Florida, Mom imagined cool summers and old friends. "It's just that I am so comfortable there," she said. When she started to cry, I wrote in my diary, "I feel like I am her rib."

I assembled a crew. Willson Powell was a friend who created charming environments. A decorator with bigger fish to fry than my project, he took it on for a modest fee and the fun of our trips to the Connecticut shore together. I can't remember how I found the contractor Ed Jennings, but he must be out of business since he finished everything on time for a fair price and never disappeared. The landscape artist JoAnne Greenwood (seriously) brought lilac trees, mounds of grasses, daisies, and day lilies, turning the plain backyard into an English garden.

The author at her new house in Knollwood.

The walls and paneling came down. The now-open great room was painted coffee with OW-18 off-white trim and carpeted wall-to-wall in butterscotch. French doors marked the entrance to the porch, its floor lined in green sisal. The plush-white carpets, which Willson chose for the bedrooms, gave them an unlikely aura of luxe. Then a huge moving van came, and Mom, age 86, stood supervising beside it. I had inventoried her Florida furniture and chose only what I liked for Neptune Drive. The first foray of our long and gentle power struggle had begun.

We both knew the not-so-golden rule of real estate: "As long as you live in my house, you live by my rules." And we both knew that the worm had turned. She was brave, canny, and determined to maintain power while physically it had begun to slip away. Mentally she never lost a beat. Bridge and crossword puzzles had done their trick, keeping her sharp of wit and tongue.

We became a couple, our relationship fraught with love, guilt, and the contemplation of matricide. I went back and forth to New York, leaving her alone sometimes for several weeks. I was dating (would it never end?), and gentleman callers occasionally spent the night. Mom would make her imperious face of disapproval, well honed from years of teaching. She would sulk off to her room where her deafness and the hum of the tiny TV by her bedside spared her from the worst.

She rebelled against her increasing dependency on me by biting my hand. "Well, your IQ is not as high as your brother's," she proffered. According to Mom, my "gourmet" recipes were "for the birds." So I made her great recipe for tomato soup cake, presenting it proudly. She looked at it (as only she could) down her nose. It was not quite right. Here's the recipe:

Tomato Soup Cake

Mix:

½ cup butter

1 cup white sugar

1 well-beaten egg

½ teaspoon cloves

½ teaspoon nutmeg

½ teaspoon cinnamon

Add alternately:

2 cups sifted flour

1 teaspoon baking soda

1 teaspoon baking powder

1 can Campbell's Tomato Soup

¾ cup raisins, floured

Beat well together. Bake at 350 degrees for 40 to 45 minutes.

Contradictions abounded in our psychological terrain. She told me, "I don't approve of your life." She told a friend, "Jane always dates losers." Unsurprisingly I shied away from confidences. "You shut me out," she lamented. She complained that she must walk on eggshells when I

Mom's Tomato Soup Cake recipe, in her own hand.

was in the house—my house. Then she claimed that she had too many responsibilities keeping the house running. Her house.

I developed strategies to get away from Mom, the best of which was the garden. I would weed, prune, dig, mulch, and plant while Mom murmured admiration at my industry. I would take extra time at the supermarket buying her weekly supply of butter, sugar, coffee, rotisserie chicken, and biscuits. I would write in my diary, pretend to have office work to do, and take long walks along Maple Avenue to Fenwick.

When I came in tired after three hours on the Metro North and Shoreline East from New York City, she would be longing to talk. As her world contracted, her attention to detail expanded. She would be eager to tell me that Helen Cuozzo's son from the West Coast was visiting her; Carl Dahlberg had a procedure; she had a card from

Ginny and a long, news-filled letter from Bea, and Bart had called yesterday morning.

In the first few years at Neptune Drive, Mom continued her lifelong commitment to Tide detergent and doing the laundry on Mondays. She was a big fan of polyester pants suits (washable) and open-toed shoes even in winter (a fashion trend well understood by most women over 70). Her laser-eyed dirt detection gift continued well past her cataract operations. She continued to drive to town for her weekly wash and set, shrinking slowly behind the wheel of her big Buick.

Pushing 90, she started to gather a team of her own. Michael and Glenna became the children she should have had—listening to her advice, living around the corner, and helping with various chores. She hired a cleaning team that had also worked for Art Carney when he lived in Westbrook. "He called them Spic and Span," she laughed. Finally she found Margaret McLeod when she needed more caring. With her slight brogue, gentle manner, and strong arms, Margaret stayed with Mom until the end.

Mom spent many days alone on Neptune Drive, yet right next door was Norma Bradford, who was also a lady from Maine living alone in a little house in Old Saybrook. They never shared a meal. Mom tracked Norma as her car backed in and out on errands to the library or the store. "She is a busy one," said Mom. They both loved the Red Sox and assiduously followed the games on TV. Each on their own couches, they would phone one another to commiserate on the score.

Mom was also the life of the party. I had festive dinners and weekend guests. My New York colleagues, the staff of the City Opera fundraising department, gathered for retreats. Mom made cameo appearances. I can see her standing at the French doors, pretending to be on her way to an early bedtime, lured to the long table on the porch by my friends who had poured in, delighted to discover Old Saybrook was more than just an Amtrak stop on the way to Boston.

One winter weekend a group of us gathered for the eagle watch. Eagles had famously, majestically, thrillingly, returned to the Connecticut River in recent years, and the Deep River Steamship Company ran trips led by eagle-eyed (apologies) naturalists. No better excuse for carrying a flask was ever had. We were joined by locals

Lunch party with Mom and celebrity guest Heywood Hale Broun.

with New York roots. The ever-glamorous Helen Weber wore a fly-fishing vest. Connie Treadwell, a leader of the Ivoryton Playhouse board, as always wore spikey high heels. Back on Neptune Drive, the supper, chilling in the refrigerator, took hours to heat. The long cocktail hour made for an especially memorable day.

I needed to make a life for myself in Old Saybrook. My anchors were Roddy and Laurel O'Connor, who grew up at Old Lyme Shores and, like me, had left for New York and returned to the Connecticut shore. When they lived on Joshua Town Road in Hadlyme, I would brave the long, dark drive back to Old Saybrook, imagining deer in my headlights at every turn but comforted by their friendship.

I met Keith Green at the railroad station, carrying a huge plant, looking harmless, and looking for a ride. I followed his directions up the drive to one of the grandest houses in Old Lyme, which Keith and his wife, Candy, called "Rooster Hall." It was fun to be one of their many friends who cheered as they succumbed to the lure of innkeeping, virtually a disease on the Connecticut shore.

Café Routier was my local. The original Routier, French for "truck stop," was located on the curve where Route 1 meets 154 in Old Saybrook. (Now it is Rosemary & Sage.) I would sit with Mom for her 5:30 supper, watch *Wheel of Fortune* and *Jeopardy* on TV with her, then slip off to enter the little bar directly through the restaurant's back door. The beloved classics—trout, steak-frites, and Mom's meatloaf—were already on the menu. I seldom ate alone, as couples who had swung off I-95 on their way to Chester or Stonington became my dinner companions.

Like Mom, I felt comfortable and safe in Old Saybrook. There was so much there to love. I could swim off the Knollwood pier. I found a tennis teacher who coached me on the high school court and went to tennis clinics at the Old Saybrook Racquet Club. I bought a kayak at North Cove Outfitters. I joined the pool at the Inn at Saybrook Point. I went to antique fairs, rummage sales, and to the library. I never made a new friend. Old Saybrook is a family community not too welcoming of single women from away.

Luckily my own tiny family was expanding by one. Still living on Long Island, Bart and his wife, Linda, had brought forth a baby girl, wrapped her in a nylon blanket (it was August in the year 1995), and named her Sarah. Gramma D, as Mom soon became known, could hardly manage the ferry and long drive. So my brother sent a plane. Bart had a pilot friend with a single-engine Beechcraft. They picked up Mom at the Chester airport and whisked her to Easthampton where they put her first and only grandchild into her welcoming, arthritic arms. This was the kind of courage that got Dorothy née Small Gullong a long way from Aroostook County, Maine.

It is hard for us Gullongs to leave the Connecticut shore. Within a year of Sarah's birth, Bart – and *family* (which Mom would intone in three syllables, strongly implying the superiority of this status) had moved to East Lyme. Now there were *fa-mi-ly* visits to Neptune Drive.

Mom's plane ride to Easthampton.

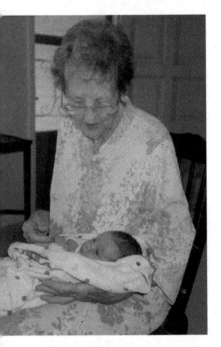

Mom with her first and only grandchild.

While usually indifferent to children, I was besotted by Sarah. "Sarah Elizabeth is coming to bring us joy, " I wrote in my diary. She is, "the incredible, adorable, laughing, running Sarah." The unsightly prefab shed in my yard became what Sarah called "our little house," where I took her for a doll house tea party. I could see her personality emerging, proud, curious, complicated, but still a little child, adorable in her new coat.

I believe that Mom lived longer and left happier having returned to Old Saybrook. For whatever we were worth, her family was around. She resumed her long-standing role as a tutor and advisor to her favorite (and only) nephew, Leonard Lieberman. Peggy Lieberman, who had cared so lovingly for her own mother, my Aunt Katie, during her last years in Chester, was nearby. On her rides down the shore, she would swing by. On his way to work, now in Berlin, Bart would swing by. How I longed to swing by.

We celebrated Mom's 90th birthday on April 6, 1999, with a big party. She shared the center of attention with her five-year-old granddaughter, there to help blow out the candles. For so many birthdays, Mom had made us angel food cakes—whipping the egg whites with a wavy hand-beater, separating the eggs, and baking it in an aluminum tube pan. I proposed using the recipe to the staff of Cloud Nine cafe, who catered the party, and they laughed.

Eventually the time comes for each of us to leave the shore. As she grew fragile and suffered a weakening heart, Mom faced the end of her life with dignity and directness. Once there was a sigh of regret, and I said, "Mom, I thought you said you were ready to die." "I am," she replied, "but not today." She was barely able to eat but one night my boyfriend and I stood at the foot of her bed on our way out to dinner and asked if we could bring her anything. "A pupu platter," she said. "But not today," I said to myself.

Gramma D with Sarah Gullong.

Dot Gullong, 92, at home in Old Saybrook.

As if she were Augustus Caesar, among her last words to me were "Farewell, Jane, I am going." Her last request, at once startling, frightening, and wrenching, was that I get into bed with her. She was alone on Neptune Drive in Old Saybrook the night she died. I had returned to work in New York. But for the last few nights we were together, I held her tiny body in my arms—as on the day I was born, she had once held mine.

Red Right Returning

If ever I had longed to be in Old Saybrook, it was during the first few days in New York City after the September 11, 2001, attacks. I wanted to get away from the nonstop sirens and the smell of smoke still hanging over Broadway near my apartment at 21 East 22nd Street. Roddy and Laurel picked me up at the Saybrook train station. We made dinner at Neptune Drive. "We go over every detail of our thoughts and fears. We know so little about the attackers," I wrote in my diary. "We watch television endlessly. We are exhausted. We sleep badly. We wake up, and it is still true."

On Saturday I biked my usual route with tears in my eyes. I looked at Old Saybrook as my homeland, this simple American place of comfort. I rode by the beach where I hung out as a teenager, the wall where I was photographed as a child, the Castle, the cottages—the beautiful place now as vulnerable as was Dresden or Sarajavo.

Now my mother was gone, and thank goodness she missed this turning point in the world's story. She was busy haunting the house on Neptune Drive. She hated the new pink-striped slipcovers I put on the couch. She murmured that buying the white piano was crazy. I would never use it. She lamented that there was a man to whom I was not married in my bed again.

Robert Brown was collateral beauty. We met because my friends Michael and Vanessa Gruen thought that he was nice and geographically convenient, living in Stonington, Connecticut. The first time he called me, I agreed to accept his invitation to come to Stonington to watch the Fourth of July parade. Mother, then alive and well, talked me out of it. Have I mentioned how often she was right?

Later that summer, Robert came to me in Old Saybrook. Of course my prince would come at the wheel of a boat. He tied up his 22-foot Sea Dory called *Zerlina* on the face of the Dock & Dine pier. I drove from Neptune Drive in my big old Buick station wagon to meet him for the first time—in a bathing suit! Bending over the ropes, the boat rocking in the wakes of river traffic, he looked up at me and smiled. He handed me down and powered up the river to Hamburg Cove. We swam and talked and kissed. I worked for an opera company. His boat was named for the gamine maid in Mozart's *Don Giovanni*.

Robert, who was as true a love as a true love can be, lived in Stonington where we spent more and more weekends together. The time came for me to leave Neptune Drive. The house sold quickly and for a nice little profit. Robert sent me a valentine that said, "Be my love, Be my honey, We'll live on love and Neptune money." Our favorite trip on *Zerlina* was back to Old Saybrook and up the Connecticut River to Essex and then to Hamburg Cove. We would enter the mouth of the river, looking at the beautiful lighthouses and for the entrance buoy, murmuring to ourselves, "Red right returning."

For two decades our romance commuted between New York and Stonington and roamed the world with trips to exotic Bhutan, Kerala, Tobago, and Guadalupe as well as closer-by Paris, Venice, and Los Angeles. Messing around in boats was its centerpiece, cruising with the Stonington Harbor Yacht Club, trips in *Zerlina* up the Hudson River and to Maine. Robert died in June 2015 but not before returning to Old Saybrook to spend sad times with me at my brother's house on Cornfield Point, as Alzheimer's was robbing him of all that he was and all that we remembered.

By 2013 Bart was back in Old Saybrook. My brother had bought one of the houses at the top of Cornfield Point facing the sound along Sea Lane. It is a house beside one of the right-of-ways with commanding views of the sweep of beaches from Knollwood to Fenwick to the inner lighthouse and across Long Island Sound to Greenport, New York, on a clear day. F. Scott Fitzgerald would set it in a silver-blue gleam near dusk.

And there is something Gatsbyesque about my brother, as he tells everyone, "The third generation of Gullongs to have a house on Cornfield Point." Walking from his new house on the hot macadam streets toward the beach at Cornfield Point, looking over the porches and into the cottage windows, hearing the bells of the Vecchitto Italian ice truck, it seems that nothing has changed but me.

Postscript: Some Thoughts on Old Saybrook

While telling my family story, I have been trying to make sense of the place where it is set.

Cultural geographers, anthropologists, sociologists, and urban planners study why certain places hold special meaning to particular people or animals. Places said to have a strong "sense of place" have a strong identity and character that is deeply felt by local inhabitants and by many visitors.
—Wikipedia

Old Saybrook has a strong brand as the former summer home of Katharine Hepburn, for its beaches, its colonial history, and its iconic lighthouses at the mouth of the Connecticut River. But I wish that there was more access to its places and more celebration of its past. I wish that the town would make more of itself and its stories.

Old Saybrook could use a stronger sense of place and some place-making:

> *... a multifaceted approach to the planning, design, and management of public spaces. Place-making capitalizes on a local community's assets, inspiration, and potential with the intention of creating public spaces that promote people's health, happiness, and well-being.*
> *—Wikipedia*

A tone of exclusion was set in Fenwick by Katharine Hepburn with her famous sign at the entrance to her property: "Please Go Away." Kate was not warm, her star quality sharp like the facets of a diamond. Old Saybrook, like Kate, has elements of colonial New England charm and Yankee suspiciousness. Privacy, fiercely protected, casts a shadow over Old Saybrook's identity .

The Lighthouses

The two Old Saybrook lighthouses—the tall, slender, and elegant Inner Light, aka the Lynde Point Light, and the squat, spark plug–style Outer Light at the end of the breakwater—are symbols of the town. They appear on the logos of the chamber of commerce and the Acton Public Library, and the Outer Light is the most popular choice of image on the official Connecticut state license

Old Saybrook's Inner Light. (Old Saybrook Historical Society photo)

plate. Operated by the U.S. Coast Guard, the lights still serve their function as beacons, warning boaters of the sandbar at the shallow entrance to the river.

The Inner Light is clearly and beautifully visible from the causeway between Saybrook Point and Fenwick on route 154. The Outer Light can really only be seen well by boat. As they say in Maine, you can't get there from here. The lighthouses cannot be visited. Like Virginia Woolf's fictional family longing to go but never making it in *To the Lighthouse*, you and your family can never visit the iconic Old Saybrook lighthouses.

Like most lighthouses throughout the country, the property and buildings of these Old Saybrook treasures have been decommissioned and made available for sale to the public. The Outer Light was for sale for several years as part of a package deal with property on

The Outer Light. (Old Saybrook Historical Society photo)

Fenwick, a chance to buy both a house and a lighthouse. No one wanted to add a lighthouse to the already hefty maintenance costs of the "cottage," so the Outer Light alone was offered at auction to the highest bidder. Frank Sciame, a former owner of Katharine Hepburn's Fenwick house, known on Trulia as "the Hepburn estate," bought the lighthouse for $290,000. In February 2017 he said that he plans to restore it for family gatherings. At least the Sciame grandchildren will get "To the Lighthouse" and hopefully have happy memories of overnights in the tower.

The status of the Inner Light, built originally of wood on land purchased from William Lynde in 1803, is unclear. Some of its charm was lost in 1966 when the Victorian keeper's cottage was torn down and replaced by a bland, nondescript, utilitarian box. Still, the romance of the tower as a beacon of safety and welcome remains. The right to public access is ambiguous. "No Access"

Two signs posted in the borough of Fenwick.

signs are posted not by the town, which maintains the roads, but by the borough of Fenwick property owners.

Preservationists, historians, and proud citizens have banded together to save their lighthouses up and down the New England coast. They have created education programs, remembering the stories of keepers and their families—long winters, courageous rescues, lives lived by the sea. They have welcomed the public to climb the towers and picnic on the shores, to encourage the local economy and the pursuit of happiness. From Campobello Island near northern Maine to Fire Island, New York, children can clamor up dark, damp, twisting stairs and look out to sea from lighthouse lantern rooms.

To use a current phrase, "Just sayin' . . ."

Beach Town

Geographically there are two Old Saybrooks: the town and the beaches. The town is adorned with its wide, esplanade-like Main Street, marked with flags and geraniums down the middle. The town is a commercial center with mini-malls and restaurants along U.S. Route 1. Founded in 1635, there are historic houses throughout Old Saybrook on streets like Pennywise Lane, in Fenwick, and throughout the North Cove Historic District. Nearly two dozen sites are on the National Register of Historic Places, including the lighthouses.

The private beaches—among them, Knollwood, Cornfield Point, Chalker Beach, Indiantown, and especially Fenwick—are accessed and maintained by their property owners' associations and accessible only to them. There are two public beaches for Old Saybrook residents. One is called Town Beach and the other is Harvey's Beach, where a resident pass or a daily usage fee will get you a parking place for your car and a spot on the sand. Both are on Great Hammock Road.

Vanishing Old Saybrook

So much that was Old Saybrook is gone. So many places of my past and of our collective past are gone—privatized, demolished, modernized, or uncelebrated.

Our family cottage, The Breakers, on West Shore Drive, the first cottage built on Cornfield Point, disappeared in 1988. A massive, two-story house now fills our old lot beside the Cornfield Point Association beach. The Cornfield Point cottage, which my grandfather built with the help of my teenage father in 1926, survived until 2000, when it disappeared into someone's idea of a mansion.

The cottages used to be alternatives to homes. Unfinished and rustic, they created a different family dynamic—life was communal and casual. The cottages were places for play. Now with cottages enlarged, renovated, and air-conditioned, the town's beach communities are becoming more suburban.

The Castle Inn on Cornfield Point closed its doors to the public in the late 1980s. A proposal to replace it with condominiums was valiantly fought by neighbors and then turned down by the town. In the final settlement, four new homes were added to the property. The Castle itself, built originally in 1906 by George Jarvis Beach to resemble the "cottages" of Newport, became a private home once again, only its red roof still visible as a beacon for sailors and a reminder of its days of gaiety and celebration.

The historic railway station in town, once a stop for trains called the "Minute Man" or "Merchants' Limited," has now been dwarfed by a huge and charmless tower providing access to the safer, higher platforms for the Acela Express and Shoreline East trains. The little depot remains, but the stationmaster's office is stripped of its once-treasured collection of photographs of historic engines and trains. "They were banned and removed by Amtrak top brass," a station attendant told me.

The Sandbar, a spinoff from the Dock & Dine, for 20 years offered an affordable lunch or snack at Saybrook Point. It was closed and sold to the town in 1989; it is now used for public meetings and is available for rent. The Dock & Dine itself is now gone, wrecked and uprooted by Tropical Storm Irene in 2011, rebuilt, reopened, and only six weeks later destroyed again by the October 2012 Superstorm Sandy. Its future remains in doubt.

There's more. It is hard not to miss the glamour of the Pease House and the Terra Mar, even as the Saybrook Point Inn thrives and honors its past with historic photos and suites named for town founders. The movie theater in the center of town—with its pillared entrance, a rotunda frescoed with an Indian-themed mural, and an easy bike ride from the beach—closed in 2000. Thurston's, the independent women's clothing store, closed after decades of selling just what you needed for back-to-school items. The Essex Steamboat Dock Tavern's upper deck in Essex, where one could drink on the second-story porch overlooking a curve of the Connecticut River, is now a museum. The shad shacks on the drive down the shore along the river are gone.

The last Cornfield Point lightship left its mooring off Long Sand Shoals in Long Island Sound in 1957. An icon of maritime history, the red vessel and its predecessors, made obsolete by technology, were for 100 years among the most romantic sights of the Old Saybrook shore. In the 1970s some citizens of Lewes, Delaware, saved and renamed it for their own lost lightship, *Overfalls*. It is now a site for visitors and special events in a canal in Lewes, its previous Long Island Sound history all but forgotten.

Ironically, there is still a lightship left in Old Saybrook. The Cornfield Point's *LV-51* sank off the shores of Cornfield Point in April 1919. The ghostly, weathered

The Cornfield Point lightship. (Old Saybrook Historical Society photo)

wreck was found in 2000 and is now designated the state's first underwater archeological preserve. It is even harder to visit than the two lighthouses.

Telling Old Saybrook's Story

Monument Park at Saybrook Point is dedicated to remembering the history of Old Saybrook. It is a poignant and not much visited place, where history seems to have been allowed to slip away. There are fading historical plaques, but all physical evidence of what is remembered there is gone. The mysterious round-house tracks mark the terminal of the Hartford–Old Saybrook trains, discontinued in the 1950s. A statue of a founding father, Lion Gardiner, erected not by the town but by his heirs, overlooks the land where in 1635 he built a fort and family and then (somewhat like me) left for the Hamptons.

Old Saybrook might have been a college town. Yale University was founded there in 1701 as The Collegiate School with a lofty vision to train and inspire a new generation of political and religious leaders. A five-ton boulder in Cypress Cemetery marks the spot with this citation: "The First Site of Yale College, Founded 1701. Removed 1716." Why in 1716 did the school's trustees want to move from Old Saybrook and agree to take bids from other towns? Yale, like the Outer Lighthouse, seems to have gone to the highest bidder.

The ghost of the Connecticut Valley Railroad haunts the largest expanse of the 11-acre park. Where trains once ran along the Connecticut River from Hartford to Middletown to Old Saybrook, only some tracks, the round-house, and the story remain. Opened in 1871, the 44-mile route ran along the west bank of the Connecticut River four times a day, meeting steamships leaving Saybrook Point for New York City. Happily, its descendant, the Valley Railroad in Essex, provides a charming reminder with a scenic railroad ride on lovely fall afternoons. But how different a pleasure trip is from a transportation link between the inland cities to the shore.

Lion Gardiner was contracted by Governor John Winthrop, Jr. in 1635 to establish a fort and lay out a town for political exiles from England at Saybrook Point, a wilderness at the mouth of the Connecticut River. The men for whom Old Saybrook is named never came at all. Viscount Seye and Sele and Lord Brooke were patentees who never visited or lived in Saybrook, members of

British peerage, the 1 percent whose gang laid claim to Indian land and set up the Sayebrook Company.

Lion Gardiner was not only an engineer and brave soldier, but he and his wife, Mary, also gave us David Gardiner, the first European child born in Connecticut, on April 26, 1636. What's even more important, Lion was a wonderful writer, and his accounts of life at Saybrook Fort in the 1630s left a vivid picture of all that our forebears endured and instigated.

Working to lay out farms and homesteads near the fort, the colonists first faced what Gardiner called "Captain Hunger." He wrote, "I have but 24 in all, men, women, and children, and not food for them for two months, unless we save our corn field, which is two miles from home . . . " (Three hundred or so years later, my family was living in Cornfield Point on that same former cornfield, looking forward to late July when we would get the first silver queens or golden bantams from Scott's or Maynard's farm stands).

For the colonists the threat of hunger paled before the fury of the Pequot Indians. Old Saybrook's first years were lived in violence and fear. Skirmishes along the Connecticut River between settlers and Pequot Indians increased, causing at least 20 Englishmen to be killed, provisions destroyed, and warehouses burned. Gardiner recounts frightful atrocities at the hands of Pequots—ambushes, murderous arrows, and victims burned alive. In response the Massachusetts Bay Colony declared war on the Pequots. Like most wars, it was declared far from the battlefield. Gardiner protested, writing, "It is all very well for you to make war who are safe in Massachusetts Bay, but for myself and these few with me who have scarce holes to put our heads in, you will leave at the stake to be roasted."

The protection of the Old Saybrook colony was one of the sparks that ignited the eventual massacre of the Pequot tribe. An army of 80 under the command of John Mason attacked the Pequot Fort near Mystic, killing 500 or more men, women, and children. Nothing like this had occurred in New England before. Surviving Pequots were hunted down and killed, leaving the tribe virtually extinct by 1637.

Historians at the Mashantucket Pequot Museum and Research Center dispute the motivation for this carnage. But for Gardiner, it secured the Saybrook Colony. He wrote that "the Lord God had . . . blessed their design and way, so that they returned with victory to the glory of God and honour to our nation, having slain 300, burnt their fort, and taken many prisoners."

Old Saybrook was safe. After four eventful years in Old Saybrook, the town's founding father, Lion Gardiner, cast his eyes over the sound and decamped for Easthampton, Long Island. Along the way he bought an island of his own from the Montaukett Indians who lived there. His descendants continued to live on Gardiners' Island until recently.

A Last Great Place

Now at Saybrook Point at the mouth of the Connecticut River (designated one of only 15 of the "last great places" in the United States by the Nature Conservancy), there is a parking lot , an owners-only marina, and a miniature golf course. We can only imagine the past: the fort where our founding colony huddled through the first winters, the train's depot, the shad-fishing boats, the steamships, the dock, and the busy hub of travel, commerce, and international trade that was once part of Saybrook Point.

But we can also imagine a future: the boardwalk of a landscaped riverside park, a sea-to-table restaurant featuring clams, lobsters, shad, and shad roe every spring with outdoor terraces and views of the river from every seat, a seafood shack with reasonably priced take-out to eat at the picnic tables scattered under the trees, a kayak-launching ramp, dockage for Audubon Society cruises to watch eagles and osprey, and the massive annual migration of tree swallows. And music? And a dance pavilion?

You Must Be From Old Saybrook

Meanwhile, there is Old Saybrook now, imperfect, beloved by most who are lucky enough to live there, an American town, an exemplar of our democracy. A jewel in its civic achievements is The Kate, a performing arts center on Main Street, named in honor of Katharine Hepburn. Its lively music and theater programs anchor Main Street at night. During the day, the anchor is Walt's

Market grocery store, independent, the food home-made, a rare phenomenon within walking distance for many who live in town.

While Main Streets in towns throughout the country are shuttered, Old Saybrook's is lively, with pubs and coffee shops and, yes, antique stores. While Anna James, the first African-American female pharmacist in Connecticut, sold the historic pharmacy on Pennywise Lane long ago, inside and out the building looks much the same as it has for 125 years, and you can still buy ice cream at the soda fountain. Block Island swordfish and Stonington scallops are available from the Old Saybrook Fish Market on route 1, run by a fourth-generation local fishing family, the Roots.

Old Saybrook has a lively civic society. The Old Saybrook library and schools are among the best in the state. Poverty is met with compassion through the churches and the Shoreline Soup Kitchen and Pantry. The town has supported moderate-income housing. Volunteers are the engine of the town, treasuring its past at the all-volunteer Old Saybrook Historical Society, welcoming visitors to the beautiful Hart House, with its extraordinary gardens. The town government's boards and commissions are filled with committed volunteers. The Guild volunteers at the Kate work backstage, in the office, and as ushers in the aisles.

If you take it from the Facebook group "You Must Be From Old Saybrook," the town's glory is the sky, the shore, the river and the sound, its sunrises and sunsets, sandbars, and surf breaking on rocks. The 3,000 members of this affinity group post hundreds of photos reflecting the year-round natural beauty that defines life at the mouth of the Connecticut River. Most days of the year at sunset in Old Saybrook, the sky is awash with a palette of red, gold, and orange—just as it was for the Mohegan Indians, the colonists raising precious corn there, for my grandparents when they bought their little lot in the 1930s, and for my parents when they bought our family cottage two decades later.

I am from Old Saybrook, the place that Katharine Hepburn, another prodigal daughter, famously called "Paradise." And like her, I keep returning. But next time I hope to be able to go to the lighthouse.

Low tide at twilight off Town Beach, Old Saybrook. (photo by Vicki Taccardi)

Acknowledgments

I am most grateful to my brother, Bart Gullong, for his support of this project, his close reading, and for his stories. Thanks also to my cousins Peggy and Leonard Lieberman for sharing their memories, photos, and especially the boating life. Roddy and Laurel O'Connor, Gayle Morgan, Marian Godfrey, and Karen Hopkins generously read early drafts and gave me, as always, their friendship and encouragement. Thanks also to the Old Saybrook Historical Society, especially Tedd Levy.
—Jane M. Gullong

About the Author

Jane M. Gullong is a retired arts administrator and fundraiser who lives in New York City and Southampton, New York. *Dancing at the Castle* is her first book. She would welcome reader comments and shared memories of the Connecticut shore. She can be reached at:

jane.gullong@gmail.com

CPSIA information can be obtained
at www.ICGtesting.com
Printed in the USA
LVHW082126171220
674456LV00029B/660

9 780692 064580